But They're So Nice:
Unmasking Covert Abuse & Narcissistic People

*A blend of personal survivor stories, psychological knowledge,
and practical advice.*

Eleni Sagredos

Dedicated to those who've held space, listened and helped me heal, my clients and community of survivors with beautiful empathic souls and people who think this book is about them. It is.

TABLE OF CONTENTS

Chapter 20

Are They Really A Narcissist?

Chapter 21

Does it Matter?

Chapter 22

Healing From Narcissistic Relationships

Chapter 23

References, Resources & Further Reading

Introduction:
Unmasking Covert Abuse

"If they're such a nice person, why are they making me feel so bad?" is a common question from those experiencing a narcissistic relationship with a covert abuser.

While the rest of this book strives to be gender neutral I cannot ignore this phenomenon that is specific to hetero relationships with "nice" or "good" men who abuse women. These "nice guy" abusers are more insidious.

Many women are socialized to give self-proclaimed "nice guys" the benefit of the doubt, even when their behavior makes us uncomfortable or harms us. This type of man, who may call himself a feminist, a leftist, a godly man, a spiritual man, or is "working on himself" in therapy, relies on his "good guy" status as a shield from accountability.

His identity as a nice guy prevents him from reflecting on the ways in which he harms women. Unlike openly misogynistic and overtly aggressive men, the nice guy's abuse is insidious. When his partner asserts boundaries, he projects fault onto her for being "sensitive", "immature" or by twisting her perceptions to avoid accountability. He may punish her passive aggressively, under small insults disguised as corrections or jokes. He may even assert control under the guise of feminist and therapeutic talking points.

His rhetorical alignment with these more socially awakened ideologies makes her doubt her perceptions. Maybe she is damaged, maybe he is right, maybe she is being too much, too sensitive, not doing enough. In reality, no ideology a man aligns himself with inherently protects women.

Self-proclaimed male allies often use leftist language and therapy techniques to bypass accountability. To compound this, when a "nice guy" harms women he denies wrongdoing in order to preserve his "good guy" identity. This identity is so ingrained that any threat or implications to the otherwise is rejected instead of causing introspection. It is his whole identity so he cannot possibly be an abuser, right?

Additionally, others reinforce his image by blaming his wife/girlfriend/female friend etc. for "making" him act this way, never forcing him to confront his actions because they cannot fathom that the "nice guy" would be capable of abuse. Being nice becomes another performance of manhood, false chivalry and not evidence of a genuine grasp of inequality especially within hetero intimate relationships. Still, society deems even "nice" men safer than women's own perceptions. Thus, the women in these relationships self-gaslight. They learn to ignore discomfort and abuse to uphold these men's fragile identities.

When a nice guy's mask of goodness becomes a shield against accountability, women suffer. These men will often place women on a pedestal. Yet this idolization reflects his projected narrative, not our humanity. They idealize women not based on our humanity but the image and validation, and narrative we reflect back to them. If we don't fit, it's deemed our flaw, not his limited maturity. We may then internalize the ways we fall from pedestals when unable to reflect their projections.

However, these "nice guys" don't humanize their partners although they may believe they do. They place them into little boxes they can easily digest. The "strong woman" the "caretaker" or even the lesser known "manic pixie dream girl".

Their metric of a good partner is also rooted in their idea of how he wants to be perceived by other men. He may choose women based on how those men will approve or be impressed by being able to secure such partners. However these men will be unable to maintain healthy equal relationships with them because of their limited capacity to view women outside of the boxes they've created. They cannot hold space for anything outside of their crude caricature of us, unable to truly see their female partners so reject nuance and complexity.

Okay, thank you for coming to my talk. I promise the rest of this book will be as gender neutral as possible. To begin, despite gender, the "nice" abuser is always highly narcissistic. It lies in their duality, the nice persona and the harmful manipulator. This nice persona is also known as the "mask".

In the depths of our pursuit for love and connection, we often stumble upon relationships that defy our expectations and leave us bewildered. Among these intricate webs of human interaction, there exists a particularly confusing entanglement – the narcissistic relationship. It is within the grasp of these relationships that the very essence of our identity can be eroded, leaving scars that may take years to heal.

Overt manifestations of abuse lurked within the walls of my own childhood. My father, with malignant narcissistic tendencies, cast a dark shadow over our home. Behind the facade of a seemingly virtuous and godly man, he hid his physically abusive and monstrous nature. At home fear would ripple through us as he unleashed his wrath, spewing venomous words while foam formed at the corners of his mouth.

My mother escaped that oppressive marriage and of course being a godly man, few believed what she had endured. He was loved by friends and members of our community. They blamed her, that she must have done something to anger him and set him off. The betrayal made it worse. The scars she carried were not just physical but etched deep within her spirit.

Despite my intimate knowledge, I was blind to the subtle manipulations, the gaslighting, the erosion of my self-esteem. I believed that abuse only took on overt forms, like yelling, hitting, or overt name calling, unaware of the insidious nature of psychological covert abuse and coercive control. And worse of all, my experiences made me believe it could never happen to me.

We are a society marred by this collective ignorance, uneducated in the realm of covert forms of abuse like psychological abuse, emotional abuse, mental abuse, ambient abuse and what entails coercive control or power imbalances. We fail to recognize the scars that remain hidden, the bruises that don't leave a physical mark and the covert abuse and manipulation that's often so difficult to explain. It is a silent epidemic that thrives in the shadows of misconception and misinterpretation.

Speaking with friends and clinical professionals, recounting the bewildering and confusing events of my failed relationship and progressed to the cold stare my abuser gave me when I had sobbed in front of him, how he watched me break down without emotion and absolute indifference, he displayed following a duper's delight, the criticizing, berating, minimizing my feelings and withholding affection, the dramatic shift from placing me on a pedestal to a feeling that nothing I did was good enough, I couldn't help but feel a sense of relief when a friend offered an explanation.

"That's abuse. You were dating a narcissist" she said matter-of-factly. Abuse? But he never swore at me. He never hit me. He barely raised his voice. How could it be abuse? And narcissists? The term was not foreign to me, but I had always associated it with someone who simply had a big ego.

All I could pinpoint was the relationship made me feel "bad" and those interactions made me feel "small". He made me feel as though I was a child. At that time, I hadn't yet learned the terminology or what truly defines abuse. But I want to stress that if this is how you feel around a partner, that is an indication of abuse caused by manufactured power, superiority and control; the bedmark of abuse.

In the chapters that follow, we will explore the complex world of these forms of abuse and narcissistic personalities. We will delve into the intricate dynamics of what defines the cycle of a narcissistically organized relationship, the idealization, devaluation and discard phases and explore the nuanced ways covert abuse manifests within relationships.

The covert nature of these relationships is what often makes them so challenging to recognize and navigate. Narcissistic relationships can begin with alluring promises, showering us with love, adoration, and an overwhelming sense of belonging. But beneath the surface lies a complex interplay of power, control, and emotional manipulation. It is a dance that masks the true intentions of the abuser, leaving us gasping for air, searching for answers, and questioning our own sanity.

I recently came across a social post that struck a chord with me and is something that I've seen echoed by myself and my own clients. It stated, "Who was happily looking for a soulmate, but feels like they ended up with a degree in psychology, specializing in narcissistic personality disorder?"

While I've never believed in soulmates and as amusing as it was, it also carried some truth. From what I've seen, understanding and healing from these relationships often causes victims to delve into the complex realm of abuse, and even personality disorders just to grapple with and understand our bewildering experiences. Education is usually the first step into healing.

Regrettably, in the realm of clinical practice, counseling, and therapy, some professionals may encounter challenges in recognizing and comprehending the complexities of these personalities and relationships. So, unfortunately, often survivors of abuse are those that have been forced to develop a profound understanding of the mechanisms of manipulation and emotional abuse and who possess an in-depth comprehension of this intricate issue.

These individuals, through lived experiences, have acquired an intimate knowledge of the tactics employed by abusers and the profound impact on our lives along with the psychological reasoning behind these abusive and narcissistic tendencies.

The purpose of this book is twofold. Firstly, it serves as a testament all survivors possess to rebuild ourselves from the pain left behind by narcissistic relationships. Secondly, it aims to provide a compass to those who find themselves in these toxic dynamics, guiding toward a path of self-discovery, healing, and liberation.

This book is not just a means for education but a recounting and collection of stories from other survivors who I've spoken with and who have shared the intimate details of their relationships with me. Of course, the names of the individuals involved will be changed to protect their identities. This is so you can see how abuse really looks. How it begins slowly and insidiously and is often hard to recognize when you're in it.

This book serves as a powerful call to action and a comprehensive guide for those seeking to understand the intricacies of their experience, covert abuse and narcissistic relationships.

As we continue on, I want to thank you from the bottom of my heart. It is such a privilege to be part of your healing journey. I want to also remind you that you are not alone. There are countless others who have faced the same struggles, battled the same demons, and emerged stronger on the other side. By sharing our stories and arming ourselves with knowledge, we raise awareness and encourage a society that recognizes and rejects abuse of all forms.

May this book serve as a guiding light in the darkness, illuminating the path toward healing, self-love, and a future free from the grip of narcissistic relationships.

Chapter 1

Was It Abuse?

"Covert narcissism is the worst and most insidious form of narcissism because the abuse is so hidden. Most people don't even realize they are being abused when they are in these relationships."
— Debbie Mirza

To begin, if you find yourself asking the question "Was I in an abusive relationship?" it's crucial to reflect on why. In a truly healthy and supportive relationship, you wouldn't feel the need to constantly question your partner's actions or try to rationalize their behavior. If you find yourself seeking explanations, reassurance, validation, looking for answers, or for example desperately googling things your partner has said or done to you attempting to make sense of your partner's behavior towards you it's a huge indicator the relationship is not genuinely healthy and nurturing. A fulfilling relationship should provide a sense of security, love and care for your emotional well-being. If this question arises, it suggests that your intuition is sensing something amiss.

An abuser can be defined as someone who inflicts cruelty or harm upon another. Expanding on this definition, an abuser is an individual who repeatedly seeks to assert control in the power dynamics of intimate relationships.

When I mention abuse, I include any behaviors or attitudes intended to intimidate, belittle, control, manipulate, emotionally or psychologically hurt, or physically harm someone all within the dynamics to exert power, manufactured superiority over and control of another's behaviors.

Identifying and acknowledging abuse can be an intricate and nuanced process, often devoid of clear-cut markers. At times, it may manifest as a lingering feeling that something is amiss within the relationship, engendering confusion and uncertainty. It is crucial not to dismiss these intuitions or wave them off as insignificant, merely because they do not align with conventional portrayals of abuse involving overt physical violence, yelling, or name-calling. The reality is that the landscape of abuse is far-reaching and multifaceted, encompassing a myriad of complexities that can be challenging to define.

We assume abuse only involves aggressive behaviors like physical violence or verbal assaults. However, abuse can take subtler forms that are equally harmful. Tactics like gaslighting, emotional manipulation, and other means of psychological control can deeply undermine a victim's self-worth and agency. Though the signs may not be as overt, the emotional damage inflicted can be just as severe. It's important not to trivialize or invalidate these more covert abusive behaviors. All forms of abuse, whether overt or subtle, should be taken seriously.

You can detect when someone is speaking down to you. There's observable body language and a condescending tone of voice. Don't ignore these more subtle belittling gestures. Covert abuse erodes a victim's self-esteem through tactics like constant criticism, manipulating, emotional withdrawal, micromanaging, belittling, degrading all while using body language to convey superiority, disgust or anger. These tactics leave the victim feeling anxious, confused, depressed, all while self worth is diminished insidiously by the abuser. Unlike overt physical violence or verbal aggression, covert abuse relies on more understated tactics to gradually undermine a victim's confidence, perception of reality, and sense of self-worth.

On the surface, incidents of covert abuse may seem insignificant or trivial when looked at individually. However, it is the persistent, insidious nature of these recurring incidents that inflicts severe psychological and emotional damage over an extended period of time. A major difficulty in identifying covert abuse stems from the abuser's ability to carefully disguise their manipulative behaviors behind claims of love, charm, or feigned ignorance.

Abusers will present their twisted narrative with absolute conviction and confidence, making it extremely challenging for the victim to recognize the abuse. Many victims only realize they were being abused long after the relationship has ended, in what is termed "delayed realization."

The abuser systematically chips away at the victim's perception of reality, making them feel insecure, flawed, and compelled to constantly apologize and walk on eggshells. The victim is made to believe the issues in the relationship are their fault alone. They begin to doubt their own instincts and adopt the abuser's version of events, even when it goes against their gut feelings.

This is why I urge those experiencing covert abuse to look beyond superficial explanations and trust your intuition when something feels wrong or "off" in the relationship. It means noticing patterns of criticism, manipulation, superiority, and emotional cruelty that signal an imbalance of power. Small incidents may not seem profoundly harmful by themselves, but the cumulative effect of these recurring behaviors over months or years can be extremely detrimental.

Abusers often utilize multiple tactics of manipulation and control that compound each other's effects over time. We need to consider the relationship holistically, looking for patterns of power and control. This wider lens allows us to better recognize abuse in all its forms and complexity.

Abusers who utilize covert abuse can be masters of deception. They hide their controlling behavior beneath a charming, caring facade. Through convoluted logic and distortion of reality, they gradually cause victims to doubt their own perceptions. Their manipulation arsenal combines outright lies with subtle physical cues that reinforce the false narratives. Victims may find themselves slowly accepting the abuser's version of truths, even when it contradicts their gut instincts. This form of psychological abuse erodes a victim's ability to trust their inner voice. When aspects of a relationship leave you feeling confused, unsafe, or deeply unsettled, it's important to trust your inner voice.

In the early stages of abuse, victims will often make excuses for their abusive partner's behaviors, taking the blame upon themselves or believing they are the cause of issues, as the abuser intends for them to feel. This manipulated sense of self-blame stems from the confusion of being unable to conceive that a loved one could be intentionally meaning to psychologically and emotionally harm. In reality, significant levels of covert abuse can remain tragically undetected for months, years or even decades.

Despite growing awareness, misconceptions still surround domestic violence and prevent survivors from getting help. Harmful narratives downplay experiences and wrongly suggest support isn't warranted. There is also a concerning lack of education on the dynamics of power imbalance, coercion and control that enable abuse. To truly address this issue, we need more nuanced conversations that don't rely on stereotypes. Domestic violence comes in many forms, and we must strive to understand them all to provide meaningful support.

Examples of covert abuse may include continuous criticism, one sided power plays, belittling, manipulation, emotional unkindness or jokes made at your expense. While these may not appear deeply harmful individually, their persistent and callous nature, combined with the difficulty in identifying and avoiding them, leads to significant psychological deterioration. This type of abuse is often described as death by one thousand paper cuts. The impact of this behavior on your mental well-being becomes substantial, as it erodes stability, induces anxiety, and exacerbates mental decline.

The numerous subtle yet significant patterns can leave someone feeling perpetually inadequate and "not good enough." This situation is far more precarious than it may seem initially, as it can lead a person to internalize a belief that they are inherently flawed.

Furthermore, abusers do not abuse all the time. They sprinkle good times, loving gestures in between the abusive behavior. The persistent damage stems from the overall patterns of manipulation and control woven through the relationship. The story of abuse often lies in recognizing those patterns. Identifying and naming the complex manipulation tactics is empowering for victims, allowing them to trust their instincts, regain agency, and take steps toward safety and freedom.

Chapter 2

"They're So Nice"

"Narcissism isn't a diagnosis, actually the word narcissism is a noun. The word narcissistic is an adjective. These are descriptive terms..."

-Dr. Ramani Durvasula

You know who else was reportedly "nice"? Ted Bundy. A friend of his, Marlin Lee Vortman, said "He was a very nice person" and that he was "the kind of guy you'd want your sister to marry." His own family didn't suspect his murders. His mother was adamant that there was no way he committed those atrocities.

My own experience and through the stories from coaching clients opened my eyes to a new breed of abuser—the covert "nice" abuser. Lundy Bancroft highlights this type of abuser in his book "Why Does He Do That?". These abusers can be any gender. However, what they all have in common is that these abusers possess the ability to appear gentle, kind, charismatic, and even empathetic, vulnerable, or sorrowful. It is precisely this facade that renders their abuse so insidious and bewildering, making it exceedingly difficult for those ensnared in such relationships to detect the toxicity lurking beneath the surface.

These abusers can go undetected by their friends and family for decades. They can be pillars of the community. They look just like everyone else, making people unaware that monsters walk among us. They do not fit the generalized description of an angry or violent abuser. This facade often attributes to the victim further isolating because they feel that they will never be believed.

This abuser manipulates perceptions, often presenting themselves as loving partners, who just tried their best and have no idea why the victim is saying these horrible things about them such as claiming abuse. They may excel at maintaining a positive image, projecting an outward persona of generosity, empathy, and respect. These abusers are skilled at selectively choosing moments to display their unpleasant side, creating confusion and doubt for their victims.

Behind the façade of "nice," a deeply disturbing truth lurks, concealed from the public eye. Often the victim is so confused by the change in behavior, reinforced by intermittent reinforcement of love and kindness between the disrespectful behavior that they do not speak up during the relationship, as the covert abuser has convinced the victim that what is happening is their fault and is normal which causes victims to feel shame.

When confronted, abusers often deny their abusive behavior. They might say, "What I did wasn't abusive" or "I never abused you." This response is actually the opposite of how someone who truly cares about someone's experience would react. Let's examine this more. If a person calls out a pattern of abusive behavior to someone who genuinely doesn't intend to harm them, the response would be quite different. The caring individual would likely say, "I had no idea you were experiencing things this way. I am so sorry. I had no idea I was impacting you so negatively. How can I fix this? How can I apologize?"

Much like how a police department cannot conduct an impartial investigation into its own misconduct, an abuser faces a similar challenge when attempting to objectively assess their own abusive behaviors. So, when an abuser responds with, "I don't see my actions as abusive" they are not only invalidating the victim's experience but essentially making themselves the judge and jury over what constitutes abuse.

They are claiming authority to determine whether their own behavior is abusive or not. When someone endeavors to position themselves as the sole authority over their actions, they inadvertently invalidate the experience of the person they've harmed and adopt an entitled stance. This not only hinders meaningful accountability but also disrupts the victim's healing process.

To elaborate on this, what does an abuser look like? What does a covert abuser look like and who are these individuals? The spectrum of these abusers encompasses a wide array of relationships, reaching beyond the stereotypical notions we may have. They hold any title within the intricate web of human relationships. They could be your friend, sibling, cousin, romantic partner, coworker, teacher, doctor, lawyer, therapist, pastor, or parent. It is essential to recognize that the face of a covert abuser is not limited to any specific category, and understanding their prevalence across different relationships is crucial in shedding light on the extent of this issue.

Unbeknownst to many, the covert abuser skillfully conceals their aggression beneath a thin veneer of congeniality. Covert abusers are usually keenly aware that overt aggression will expose their true nature and intentions, so they prefer to keep their aggression hidden. Manipulating and controlling under the guise of love, concern, logic or even while issuing a smile. This allows them to maintain the façade of being a good person while simultaneously manipulating, intimidating, and controlling you to comply with their desires. This enables them to commit acts of aggression while evading detection.

The fabric of a relationship with a covert abuser is woven through abuse and passive aggression, giving the abuser power and control without you realizing it. They employ various subtle tactics, from disguised insults to covert manipulation to get what they want. They skillfully gain the upper hand, leaving a person feeling confused and easier to mold.

Abusers often feign ignorance or stupidity. But do not be fooled. The abuser is not stupid. The abuser must maintain their charming and winning persona, not only to keep the people they harm from leaving but also to maintain their image with outsiders. They know that if outsiders could see what is really going on behind closed doors and if their victim caught on to the abuse, they might run the risk of being called out or shunned. They also know that if outsiders think they are a great person, they are more likely to support them rather than the victim.

Some of their maneuvers are so imperceptible that they are nearly undetectable, allowing them to easily refute any accusations of wrongdoing. Their victim's instincts may signal that something is amiss in the relationship, but without concrete evidence, they find themselves perpetually questioning and second-guessing their feelings.

A covert abuser may come across like they are hurt by their victim's words and accusations of abuse or are concerned about their mental health for even thinking such things about the abuser. Their explanations appear logical and sound, which makes it all the more difficult for a person who experiencing this to see what's really happening. They are finely attuned to people's weaknesses and know just how to use them to their advantage. They will twist things around so that the abuser's behavior seems to be the other person's fault.

Some of the best abusers never raise their voice or act out physically. However, the depths of their manipulation can be one of the most destructive behaviors because it causes the victim to question and lose confidence in themselves.

This all being said, it's understandable to question and be confused if all the manipulation and abuse caused by covert abusers is calculated and malicious. Of course, as this is precisely the intent of covert abusers who use tactics to feign ignorance and plausible deniability.

So "What if they don't know what they're doing?" is a common question amongst people who have experienced this form of psychological abuse.

This may be controversial but, possibly. But let me be

very specific here, they **do** know what they are doing yet some covert abusers may not acknowledge their own abusive behavior and label it *as abuse*. Consequently, they may interpret their actions as necessary, warranted, or justified.

Narcissistic "nice" and covert abusers typically have limited empathy and struggle to understand and acknowledge the feelings and experiences of others. Their focus is primarily on self and fulfilling their own needs. This self-centeredness often blinds them to the consequences of their behavior on others, including the infliction of emotional and psychological harm. In short, they may not notice and if they do they may not care as they believe the victim deserved it, it was "tough love" or justify away their behavior.

As such their behavior is driven by a skewed perception of reality. They may distort reality, shifting blame onto others or minimize the impact of their actions. By distorting the narrative, they reinforce their own self-image as faultless, further blurring their understanding of their abusive behavior.

It is essential to note that this does not excuse or justify their actions. The harm caused by their behavior is real. The impact of the behaviors themselves matter most when evaluating a toxic relationship dynamic. People often believe that if abusive behavior is unconscious or unintentional, it somehow doesn't qualify as abuse. This is where many individuals stumble, particularly those who engage in abusive behavior. They may argue, "Well, I didn't know what I was doing was abusive".

Whether or not a person uses abusive behavior, the majority of individuals lack a comprehensive understanding of what abuse truly entails. Therefore, some individuals using abusive behaviors are unaware that their actions fall within this category. They use tactics of abuse, knowing they are attempting to manufacture power and control to elicit a specific action from you. So while they might recognize that they are achieving their goals through certain behaviors they've learned, they often fail to contextualize these actions as abusive or as part of a power dynamic.

However, regardless of their awareness, the impact of their behavior remains abusive. The priority should be caring for one's own health and protecting against further harm. I urge you not to focus on why the behavior exists to determine if you should tolerate it. The behavior is enough.

Do not focus on intent but rather impact. We cannot go into an abuser's mind to definitely know without a shadow of a doubt that their behavior was not highly intentional.

Additionally many will then try to over explain to the abuser that these toxic tactics and maladaptive behavior is abuse. Do not try to convince them they are abusive. They often do not care as these maladaptive methods have always garnered results.

While it may seem like explaining to then will help the situation, after all, relationships are about communication right? This is only the case in healthy non-toxic and not abusive relationships. Instead of accountability and repair abusers commonly debate with you or manipulate you during these moments intended for communication and vulnerability. They may say their behavior was not intentional, so it was not harmful. When you encounter individuals who attempt to engage you in a debate about their motives, it's important to recognize that this tactic serves as a form of manipulation. The intention behind their actions holds minimal significance when it comes to how their behavior affected you. Engaging in such discussions creates a dangerous division between your perception and actual experience, effectively absolving them of accountability for their actions.

The abuser's strategy involves presenting their intentions to someone they've harmed, expecting that person to adjust their perception based on the abuser's stated motives. This manipulative approach not only distorts perception of those they've harmed but also is intended to reshape the entirety of their experience. As a result, their victim's genuine experience is invalidated, leaving them with the belief that they misinterpreted events due to the abuser's intentions, thereby making their victim question the validity of their reactions.

This tactic falsely portrays the abuser's intentions as equalizers over their victim's foundational perception, which forms the basis of their experience. This convoluted dynamic creates a psychological rift within the person the abuser harmed, separating the harmed party's inner emotional state from the external occurrences. Over time, this disconnection can lead to detachment as a response to the inflicted trauma.

This is precisely why, in situations where you hold others accountable, it's important to reject discussions about their intentions. These conversations only serve to validate *the perpetrators'* emotions and egos. Such exchanges revolve around their self-image and how they desire to be seen. Disregarding their intentions might distort their self-image, potentially casting themselves in an unfavorable light. Consequently, they rush to rectify their image, steering the interaction according to their desires and objectives. Needless to say, this approach is far from constructive. Hence, it's essential to firmly oppose engaging in debates about intentions. Some might label this as inflexible or unreasonable, but this stance arises from a deep understanding of the manipulation and psychological harm that such discussions can lead to. Allowing these debates shifts the focus toward soothing the psychological abusers' emotions, overshadowing the genuine impact of their actions.

Additionally while we may feel sympathy, and excuse the abuse because the abuser may have had a difficult childhood we must refrain from this train of thought. Yes, while it's generally thought that specifically NPD (Narcissistic Personality Disorder) may be caused by significant trauma in their developmental years, spoiling, over indulgence or a genetic predisposition may also be the root cause. Additionally, there is no proven tie between trauma and abuse in abusers without pathologies. So, regardless of origin, chronic abusive and narcissistic patterns, thought processes, and maladaptive abusive coping mechanisms are not a justification for abuse. Period.

Chapter 3

Psychological & Covert Abuse

"Plausible deniability is the covert narcissist's greatest weapon in their arsenal of gaslighting tools."

– Debbie Mirza

Are you bringing up an issue but always finding that you're the one who ends up apologizing by the end of the discussion? Do you often feel confused, depressed or that your self-esteem is just not what it once was before the relationship? Does your partner talk down to you, reprimand, belittle or criticize you? Are you aware that something isn't right about your relationship, but can't quite put your finger on what it may be? Are they indifferent to your pain, emotions or even tears?

You may be experiencing psychological abuse.

"Death by a thousand paper cuts" is a metaphor often used to describe narcissistic and covert forms of abuse like coercive control, psychological and emotional abuse. It refers to a pattern of subtle, repetitive, and cumulative actions or behaviors that gradually erode a person's well-being, self-esteem, and sense of self. Each individual action may be subtle, disguised, or easily dismissed by the abuser or others, making it challenging for the victim to recognize and address the abuse. In this chapter, I will often refer to all these forms of abuse as "covert abuse". As such, covert abuse refers to a form of psychological and emotional manipulation and control that is subtle, concealed, and often difficult to recognize when you're experiencing it. Covert abuse, hidden abuse, and passive-aggressive abuse are all phrases used to describe psychological and emotional abuse typically employed by narcissistic abusers and can be difficult to detect because they are subtle and often occur in non-physical ways.

As this behavior isn't extreme, covert abuse may be difficult to detect within a relationship, because while it can be observable, isolated instances may appear as insignificant to the person experiencing it. Although this distinction may seem minor, it does become significant when one experiences it on a regular basis.

In a psychologically abusive relationship, every perceived imperfection is subjected to relentless scrutiny. Over time, the victim internalizes this critical perspective, self-examining even the most minor shortcomings.

Consequently, they harshly self-criticize for the slightest mistakes, gradually adopting the abuser's distorted viewpoint. As the onslaught of criticism becomes routine, the victim's self-esteem diminishes, leading their partners to accept these false allegations as truth.

Psychological abusers skillfully cultivate an atmosphere of perpetual anxiety and a pervasive sense of inadequacy. Initially, they might have praised the victim's vibrant personality, only to later chastise them for being too exuberant. When the person the abuser has harmed seeks closeness and intimacy, suddenly the abuser may say they have become "too much" for the abuser's liking. Should the victim make an effort to enhance their appearance, the narcissistic abuser cynically mentions it must be due to the victim's low self-esteem. Every facet of the victim's identity and actions becomes subject to relentless criticism and scrutiny in the web woven by the psychological abuser.

Ambient & Covert Abuse:

Ambient abuse is a psychological abuse tactic aimed at implanting foreign ideas or feelings into the victim's mind while skillfully concealing the abuser's true intentions. Think of it as an advanced form of gaslighting that is more difficult to detect. Ambient abuse stands as a form of manipulation, creating an oppressive environment of fear and anxiety.

The ultimate aim of ambient abuse is to assert control over the victim by systematically eroding their sense of self-worth. Gradually, the covert abuser chips away at their victim's self-confidence, leading victims to doubt the truth and objective reality.

Through manipulation he covert or narcissistic abuser ensures the victim remains ensnared, ensuring a continuous supply of narcissistic validation and control.

Ambient abuse takes shape through five distinct manifestations: disorientation, rejection, shared psychosis, withholding of information, and control by proxy.

This abuser rarely exhibits irritable behavior or presents themselves as a villain. Their proficiency lies in veiling their covert abuse as acts of benevolence, designed to disarm the victim and gain their trust, thereby facilitating easier manipulation. For example, instead of directly stating, "I hate your hair like that", the covert abuser will fabricate scenarios or drop subtle hints like, "Are you sure you want to wear your hair that way?". Or instead of "I hate when you wear makeup. You should stop wearing makeup." they will instead say "You know how many chemicals are in makeup, right? I'm just looking out for you."

The abuser skillfully disorients the victim to the extent that the victim starts blaming themselves for everything that goes awry. The abuser might even adopt the role of a victim, guilt-tripping the real victim when questioned about their motives. The outcome is the target perpetually residing in a state of self-doubt and anxiety while constantly trying to please the abuser and mold to their preferences.

These strategies are carefully designed to implant the abuser's ideas and preferences into their victim's mind, making the abuser's target to slowly believe that these thoughts and perceptions about themselves are their own, resulting in profound and incredibly effective manipulation.

The toxicity of covert abuse may thrive in the household, where the abuser perpetuates a climate of unrelenting fault-finding and high expectations. Covert abuse, ambient abuse and manipulation is akin to placing a poisonous fog in your home. The poisonous fog silently and insidiously seeps into every nook and cranny slowly harming those in the vicinity. It is incredibly difficult to identify, as it slowly and incrementally begins to permeate through every aspect of a person's life without the fog being overtly noticeable.

For instance, they may continuously disparage the victim's housework efforts, dismissing them as inadequate or not up to a certain standard deemed as "proper." The abuser moves the goalposts, and constantly finds fault, ensuring that the victim knows. No matter how earnestly they strive to meet their abuser's demands, the abuser will insist they are not doing enough and if they are they are not doing something properly. By doing so, the abuser diminishes the victim's ability to trust their own judgment, perpetuates a sense of inadequacy and creates a state of constant anxiety where the victim becomes fearful and hypervigilant to avoid more scrutiny.

Unlike overt abuse, which involves blatant acts of aggression or harm, ambient abuse, manipulation and covert psychological abuse operates through more subtle and insidious means. It involves creating an oppressive and toxic environment that chips away at the someone's self-esteem, confidence, and sense of reality.

With an air of superiority, a person enacting covert abuse artfully points out the flaws and shortcomings of their partner, framing them as the instigators and the cause for all the relationship issues. If the victim would just behave a specific way, if they would be less of this or more of this the abuser would not mistreat them. This psychological manipulation leaves their victim grappling with confusing emotions and a sense of responsibility for the turmoil, all orchestrated by the seemingly well-intentioned abuser.

The target of this abuse, naturally inclined to believe in the abuser's fundamental ethicality and the importance of cooperation and compassion as collective moral imperatives, willingly embraces a collaborative effort to address difficulties. The ambient abuser however uses this positive projection to exploit this predisposition. Should the target dare to question the intermittent barbs and disparagement of the stealth abuser, further manipulation and distortion follow suit. A bewildering narrative unfolds, casting the target as the one responsible for doubting the abuser's motives and sincerity, creating a disorienting scenario where the target is convinced that they are the ones being abusive and irrational.

They Imply That You're Stupid

A telltale sign of covert and ambient abuse is when the victim feels intellectually diminished in the abuser's presence. It's not necessarily that the abuser explicitly calls their partner stupid, but rather that the one experiencing the the abuser may subtly undermine the victim's confidence by dismissing their comments as obvious or responding with derisive looks, exasperated sighs, or subtle remarks, causing the victim to feel humiliated and reluctant to express their thoughts openly.

Within the complex interplay of the relationship, the abuser adeptly exploits the victim's perceived lack of understanding during conversations, deftly maneuvering the narrative to place the blame squarely on the victim's shoulders for any communication breakdown. However, upon closer examination, it becomes evident that the root cause lies in the abuser's own inadequate or vague explanations, skillfully obfuscated by their artful manipulation. This calculated maneuver is aimed at leaving the victim emotionally wounded and plagued with doubts about their capacity to comprehend the abuser's intentions, thereby serving as a potent tool for them to maintain unwavering control and power over the victim's perceptions.

They Talk Down To You

The covert abuser consistently assumes an air of superiority. The abuser adopts a condescending or patronizing tone when speaking. They adopt an air of self-righteousness, as if they possess more knowledge or authority, and often resort to explaining even the simplest concepts as if speaking to a small child. Such behavior is deeply insulting and belittling, leaving a person feeling demeaned and invalidated.

Their manner of communication may take on a deliberately slow pace, speaking slowly as if doubting someone's ability to comprehend what is being conveyed at a normal speed. Additionally, they may exhibit an excessive sense of poise, assuming a stance that suggests they are in a position of authority.

This calculated behavior is meant to subtly exert power and create an air of superiority, leaving the victim feeling invalidated, scrutinized and uncertain about their own thoughts and expressions. By adopting these manipulative tactics, the abuser seeks to maintain a position of power and dominance in the relationship, further obscuring the true nature of their intentions.

The impact of this demeaning behavior is not limited to significant issues but also extends to seemingly trivial matters, which, though seemingly inconsequential, can inflict profound emotional hurt. Even when their partner expresses a simple and undeniable fact, the abuser will vehemently oppose it, persistently driving home their contrary view. This unwavering insistence on negating the victim's stance, serves as a clear message that their opinions are deemed unworthy and untrustworthy in the abuser's eyes.

Moreover, when engaging in debates or disagreements with them, the victim will notice the abuser's inability to agree to disagree. Instead of respecting differing opinions, they adamantly insist on being right and refuse to entertain alternative perspectives. This rigid and inflexible stance not only creates an atmosphere of hostility but also highlights the dangerous aspect of their character, as they believe they can never be in the wrong.

In these situations, the abuser reveals their unwillingness to share in another's motions and their inclination to assert dominance over a person's thoughts and feelings. Their behavior undermines the foundation of a healthy relationship built on mutual respect, empathy, and safe communication.

They Make You Feel Unwanted

The covert and ambient abuser wields disinterest and annoyance as powerful instruments of manipulation. During their partner's sincere attempts to engage them in meaningful discussions, the abuser deploy eye-rolling and a facade of disinterest, making it clear their unwillingness to partake in the dialogue or address certain sensitive matters. This calculated demeanor is designed to both silence their partner when they dare to confront them about pressing issues and erodes the target's self-confidence when trying to communicate intimate facets of their partner's life, goals, and aspirations.

By employing this covert tactic during vulnerable exchanges, the abuser crafts a poignant and emotionally devastating blow to their partner's sense of worth and emotional safety. It is in these moments when their partner shows vulnerability and openness that the abuser will choose to leverage their partner's openness as an opportunity to diminish their standing and leave them feeling invalidated and muted.

They Manipulate Your Environment

The abuser possesses a remarkable ability to construct an incessantly bewildering environment, strategically crippling their partner's faculties and coercing them to relinquish independent thinking. For example, the abuser might consistently hide essential belongings such as the phone, car keys, or purse, and then blame the victim's forgetfulness, creating a narrative that justifies the victim's perceived reliance on the abuser's "help."

In their manipulative endeavors, covert abusers frequently resort to withholding crucial information. Outside of hiding belongings, the abuser may go as far as to deliberately neglect to inform their victim about important matters, such as due dates for bills. Both scenarios are meant to cause distress in their target while they sit back and revel in knowing they have answers to their partner's distress. The intentional lack of vital information creates a scenario wherein the victim is left feeling bewildered, disempowered and unable to navigate their life without the abuser. This calculated tactic fosters a deeper sense of dependency on the abuser, perpetuating their control over their victim's decision-making processes and overall autonomy.

By keeping the victim in the dark, the abuser seeks to maintain an advantageous position of power, eroding the victim's self-reliance and fostering an unsettling reliance on the abuser's guidance. In essence, this insidious manipulation further entangles the victim in the abuser's web of control, intensifying their vulnerability and subjugation.

Overall, these tactics serve to weaken the victim's sense of self and perpetuate a state of reliance on the abuser, allowing the abuser to maintain their power and control over the victim's life.

Belittling

The covert abuser employs a seemingly lighthearted and joking manner to belittle the victim, even doing so in the presence of others, which makes their comments all the more hurtful and demeaning. Regardless of the subject matter, their words cut deep, disrespecting and undermining the victim's worth. It is crucial to note that when they're confronted about their behavior, they conveniently dismiss it as harmless banter, further invalidating your feelings and refusing to acknowledge the harm they inflict.

They Micromanage You

In a healthy relationship, trust, respect, and open communication form the foundation for growth and mutual support. Covert abusers micromanage their partners. This involves scrutinizing and exerting dominance over their thoughts, actions, and choices. Micromanagement in relationships is characterized by an overwhelming desire for control, where one partner feels compelled to criticize and judge many aspects of the other's life. It involves excessive monitoring, incessant criticism, and a lack of trust in the partner's judgment or abilities. From dictating daily routines to nitpicking trivial matters, micromanagement gradually erodes the victim's sense of autonomy and self-worth.

Micromanagement often stems from deep-seated control issues. It may be driven by their fear of losing power, insecurity, or an underlying need to feel superior.

Gaslighting & D.A.R.V.O:

Gaslighting is a common covert abuse tactic that may also be found in ambient abuse where the abuser manipulates the victim's perception of reality. By constantly denying or distorting events, the victim starts doubting their own memory, perception, and judgment. Over time, this erodes their confidence and makes them question their own sanity, leading to a significant blow to their self-esteem. D.A.R.V.O. is an acronym that stands for Deny, Attack, and Reverse Victim and Offender. It describes a common pattern of response often employed by individuals engaging in gaslighting and manipulation tactics.

D.A.R.V.O. (Deny, Attack, Reverse Victim and Offender) is a particularly insidious technique used by manipulators. Here we will explore the concept of D.A.R.V.O., its components, and provide examples to shed light on how it is employed to further the abuser's agenda.

A telltale sign of D.A.R.V.O is entering a discussion where you bring up an instance to your partner to convey how your partner is behaving in ways that bother you but following the discussion you may find that you've inexplicably ended up apologizing instead, leaving you confused and bewildered.

Here is how D.A.R.V.O may play out:

Deny: The Art of Refuting Reality

The first step in D.A.R.V.O. is denial. The gaslighter dismisses the victim's claims or experiences, aiming to make them doubt their own version of events. Examples of denial include:

- "I never said that. You must have misunderstood."

- "You're overreacting. It didn't happen like that at all."

- "I was just joking."

- "That's actually not the problem/issue."

Attack: Blaming and Shaming the Victim

The second stage of D.A.R.V.O. involves attacking the victim, shifting blame onto them to deflect accountability. The gaslighter may employ tactics such as character assassination, insults, or raising unrelated issues. Examples of attacks include:

- "You're always so sensitive."

- "The issue is actually that you never make me feel heard."

- "Why are you being so immature?"

Reverse Victim and Offender Roles: Distorting Power Dynamics

In this stage, the gaslighter skillfully reverses the roles, making themselves appear as the victim and the actual victim as the offender. This manipulative tactic serves to confuse and disempower the victim. Examples of reverse victim and offender include:

- "You're the one who hurt me. You should apologize."

- "The problem is you and [insert something they say you have done]"

- "I can't believe you would do this to me after everything I've done for you."

- "I can't believe you would think that about me."

Conflation and Distraction:

Throughout the D.A.R.V.O. process, gaslighters may use additional tactics to further confuse and manipulate their victims. These tactics include conflation, where they combine unrelated issues to divert attention, and distraction, where they shift the focus away from their own behavior. Examples of overlapping tactics include:

- "You're just like your mother. No wonder you're always causing problems."

- "Why are we talking about this? You need to focus on your own flaws."

Stonewalling:

Stonewalling or the silent treatment in relationships constitutes a covert form of emotional manipulation and abuse, wherein the abuser deliberately shuts down and refuses to engage in communication with the victim as a means of punishment or control. This behavior, often observed in narcissistically organized relationships, can inflict profound emotional damage and foster a toxic atmosphere, leading the victim to experience feelings of disrespect, guilt, powerlessness, and a sense of being rendered invisible in the relationship.

Examples of stonewalling may include:

- The abuser avoids eye contact and responds with monosyllabic answers when the victim attempts to initiate a conversation about an issue that is important to them.
- During a heated argument, the abuser suddenly walks away without explanation, leaving the victim feeling physically and emotionally abandoned.
- After a disagreement, the abuser goes completely silent for days, withholding any form of communication or acknowledgment, leaving the victim in a state of confusion and distress.

This detrimental behavior is indicative of the abuser's lack of effective interpersonal skills and emotional regulation, as they resort to passive-aggressive tactics instead of engaging in open, honest communication to address concerns or conflicts.

Dealing with the silent treatment necessitates the establishment of clear boundaries for the victim and a refusal to internalize or personalize the abusive behavior. Instead of reacting emotionally or succumbing to the urge to beg for communication, it is essential for the victim to maintain composure and not feed into the power dynamics created by the abuser.

Withholding Affection:

Covert abusers employ a tactic of withholding affection, emotional support, or love as a powerful means of manipulation and control. By depriving the victim of the essential emotional sustenance they crave and deserve, the abuser effectively creates a dark and suffocating void, where feelings of unworthiness and inadequacy take root and flourish. This calculated deprivation of love and care fosters an environment of emotional desolation, leaving the victim with a profound sense of emptiness and a haunting belief that they are inherently undeserving of love and affection.

In a twist, the early stages of the relationship often bear witness to an entirely different facade, where the abuser skillfully dons a mask of idealization and affectionate charm. During this phase, the victim is lured in by an enchanting display of love and devotion, completely oblivious to the impending emotional abyss that lies ahead. The stark contrast between the initial showering of affection and the subsequent withholding of love creates an additional layer of confusion and heartache for the victim, intensifying their feelings of unworthiness and self-doubt.

The consequence of this dramatic change of emotional starvation is a gradual erosion of the victim's self-esteem and self-worth. The victim finds themselves caught, teetering on the precipice of emotional fragility. The abuser cunningly exploits this vulnerability to further tighten their grip on the victim's psyche, maintaining control through the manipulation of their insecurities of feeling unloved.

The impact of this emotional starvation is undeniable, slowly eroding the victim's sense of self.

Projection

Projection is a common defense and tactic among covert abusers, allowing them to shift their own undesirable thoughts, beliefs, and insecurities onto those in their proximity. In the act of projection, the abuser assigns their own negative traits to their victim. For instance, when they lie, they will accuse you of being the dishonest one. If they exhibit immaturity, they will brand you as immature. Instead of taking accountability for their actions, these individuals often resort to attacking or accusing others, using it as a diversion from acknowledging their own behavior.

Triangulation

Triangulation is when the abuser subtly orchestrates a scenario where they place you in opposition to another person. The aim of triangulation is to incite negative emotions like jealousy, inadequacy, suspicion, insecurity, anger, frustration, or even outright animosity. The toxic individual accomplishes this by ingeniously manipulating a situation, circumstance, or uttering words designed to prompt you to develop certain sentiments towards the other person. This most commonly occurs between an abuser and the abuser's ex or with the abuser and who they may be currently grooming; however it can exist in other interpersonal relationships as well.

Identify Covert & Ambient Abuse

Identifying covert abuse can be challenging, which is why it's crucial to pay close attention to your feelings and experiences with the other person. If you consistently feel small, oppressed or confused in their presence, it's worth considering the possibility of being subjected to covert abuse. Key indicators include repeated questioning of your memory about events, dismissal of your opinions, and fostering doubt in your intuition and competence. Trusting your instincts and recognizing these signs can help protect your emotional well-being and enable you to address such situations effectively.

As discussed, abuse fundamentally creates an environment of fear and anxiety. To further break down the effect they have on those they are abusing let's observe the common ways covert abuse impacts the target:

Fear

Covert abusers deploy constant monitoring of the victim's activities and decisions to ensure adherence and that the victim's behavior conforms to what the abuser wants. This surveillance instills a pervasive sense of fear in the victim, as they feel constantly scrutinized and judged.

Loss of Self-Esteem

Using demeaning tactics such as scrutinizing and constant criticism, covert abusers systematically undermine the victim's self-confidence. This erosion of self-esteem leads to feelings of worthlessness and insecurity over time.

The relentless criticism instills doubt in the victim's self-worth, negatively impacting their perception of themselves both mentally and physically. As a result, they find it increasingly challenging to make decisions or take risks due to a crippling fear of failure by not meeting the abuser's expectations.

"Walking on Eggshells" Stress & Anxiety

Victims of covert abuse grapple with chronic stress and anxiety. They are constantly burdened by worries about the likelihood of further criticism from the abuser for any mistakes they make.

This persistent stress has tangible effects on physical health, leading to issues like headaches, stomach-aches, sleep disturbances, fatigue, and even suppression of the immune system.

Chapter 4

Power & Control

At its core, all forms of abuse are inherently rooted in power and control dynamics manufactured by the abuser. Whether it's emotional, physical, psychological, or any other type of abuse, the abuser employs manipulation, coercion, and intimidation to establish dominance over the victim, systematically eroding their autonomy and self-esteem. Through tactics like micromanaging, criticism, or punishment the covert abuser trains the victim to associate displeasing them with consequences. Punishment keeps the victim in a state of anxiety, constantly modifying their words and actions to appease the abuser.

This conditioning through punishment allows the abuser to gradually "mold" the victim's behavior as they desire. The victim shrinks themselves in attempts to avoid criticism, blame or anger from their partner. They change to align with what the abuser wants, surrendering their autonomy.

Control forms the second pillar of abuse. While punishment establishes dominance through consequences, control via confusion keeps victims immobilized psychologically. The abuser purposely engineers confusion by constantly shifting expectations, running hot and cold, and concealing the abuse through manipulation and plausible deniability. This state of chronic confusion, wherein victims can never predict the expectations of the abuser, whether their feelings are valid, what they've done wrong this time is profoundly disorienting. It leads victims to doubt what is real, unable to trust their perceptions. Confusion in this manner grants the abuser immense control, as victims become utterly reliant on their partner to define reality. Through these tactics abusers deliberately manufacture anxiety and uncertainty.

The Duluth Power and Control Wheel has served as a valuable tool in identifying abuse by providing a comprehensive framework for understanding the dynamics of power and control within abusive relationships, however it is lacking defining characteristics of psychological and more defined examples of covert forms of abuse.

Clare Murphy, PhD, a psychologist with a focus on abusive dynamics in relationships, sheds light on more covert forms of psychological abuse by introducing the Psychological Abuse Wheel. This innovative model expands our understanding of the dynamics of domestic violence, emphasizing the centrality of power and control as the ultimate goal.

The core of the Psychological Abuse Wheel lies in the concept of power and control, encapsulating the ultimate objective of the abuser. Unlike outbursts of anger or conflicts of interest, a sustained campaign of psychological abuse is a deliberate effort to establish dominance. While threats of physical violence may be present, psychological abuse operates independently, seeking to subjugate and manipulate the victim without relying solely on physical force.

The Duluth Power and Control wheel, which inspired Clare Murphy's model, introduced the understanding that psychological and emotional abuse reinforces physical violence and sexual abuse. Dr. Clare Murphy suggests that these forms of abuse work in conjunction to establish domination and control, but indicating that psychological abuse may not merely be a precursor or a transitory stage leading to physical violence.

The tactics found in the Psychological Abuse Wheel include:

Emotional Indifference/Unkindness - When A Partner Fails To Show Empathy

Emotional unkindness encompasses both active cruelty and passive neglect of a partner's emotional needs. It involves turning a blind eye to their desire for support, understanding, and compassion. Tactics of emotional unkindness include ignoring a partner's attempts at repair, showing little empathy for their distress like crying, withholding expressions of concern, withdrawing affection, and failing to provide care or concern during times of vulnerability or need.

When wielded, "emotional unkindness" inflicts a deep rupture of trust within a relationship and inflicts psychological and emotional harm on the victim. The warning signs become evident when a partner refuses accountability for their actions, displaying a complete absence of compassion or empathy when their significant other endures emotional turmoil or illness. Additionally, denying or minimizing the harm inflicted, or even blaming the victim for their own suffering further cultivates an environment of emotional hostility.

This form of maltreatment manifests through actions that willfully discount the partner's feelings and disregard their emotional needs.

The repercussions of enduring emotional unkindness are profound and deeply damaging to the affective foundations of a relationship. The infliction of this withholding, the absence of compassion, is battering to the spirit as it causes a mismatch between expectations for compassion and the harsh reality of emotional neglect.

Examples of Emotional Unkindness:

One example of emotional unkindness includes a partner being indifferent when the victim is expressing harm done by the other partner. Attempts to communicate are met with no sign that the abuser cared about the victim's feelings and concerns. Despite efforts to elicit caring responses, the partner's lack of empathy persists.

Another example of emotional unkindness would include a partner who exhibits no empathy for the victim's feelings, disregarding their emotional needs entirely. In a common example I've seen with myself and many clients, the victim may be crying in front of the abuser about something that the abuser has done and the abuser will watch the victim as though they are watching paint dry with no compassion or care for their hurt.

Finally, the victim could be experiencing a devastating health scare, an illness, a situation like a miscarriage or difficult pregnancy. The abuser may refuse to offer comfort and grow increasingly dismissive.

Abusers exhibiting emotional unkindness fail to provide empathy, support, understanding, or compassion in times of vulnerability and need. Their lack of emotional responsiveness and care inflicts deep wounds, leaving victims shocked at their cruelty, emotionally isolated, unsupported and psychologically harmed.

Mind Games:

Abusers who impose one-sided power dynamics reveal a troubling pattern of prioritizing control over their partner's well-being. Within this web of manipulation, they readily switch between tactics to maintain dominance.

Despite professing a desire for loving connection, these abusers view their partners as obedient subjects, dismissing their needs and perspectives. The abuser sees their own wants as paramount, even when detrimental to their partner's welfare.

The methods used to sustain control are extensive and psychologically damaging. Tactics include sowing confusion, guilt trips, persistently questioning judgment, and deceitful manipulation.

Punishing reactions surface when partners assert boundaries or withdraw. Attempts at independence are suppressed. Overtures for understanding are rejected, fueling dependence.

A stark contrast emerges between the abuser's public charm and private cruelty. While projecting an amicable facade around others, behind closed doors their emotional abuse persists unhindered.

The impact of enduring these manipulative power games is devastating. Victims are left grappling with erosion of self-worth, independence, and emotional exhaustion from the relentless psychological warfare. The abuser's priority of control over care inflicts deep damage.

Examples of Mind-Games:

An example of mind games include when the abuser makes the victim feel confused and doubting themselves due to the abuser's mixed messages and manipulation. The abuser can block the victim's attempts to clarify things, leaving them anxious and when a victim tries to discuss their concerns, the abuser acts innocent and insists nothing was wrong, making the victim question their own judgment.

Another example is when an abuser discourages the victim's interests and makes them feel guilty for pursuing them, as if the victim was damaging the abuser's ego or when an abuser frequently questions the victim's judgments of friends and acquaintances, portraying them negatively to change the victim's views. The abuser may also just outright fabricate events the victim witnessed. The abuser's lies leaves the victim constantly uncertain of the truth.

Symbolic Aggression:

Symbolic aggression encompasses a distressing form of abuse wherein the perpetrator utilizes verbal or physical gestures that carry a profound meaning or significance beyond their surface appearance.

One prevalent tactic within symbolic aggression involves the silent treatment, a form of psychological torment that can be deeply debilitating to the victim. By employing this destructive tactic, the perpetrator deliberately withholds communication, leaving the victim feeling isolated and emotionally abandoned. The silence becomes an oppressive presence, instilling a profound sense of anxiety and confusion within the victim, who may grapple with feelings of unworthiness and inadequacy.

The impact of symbolic aggression on the victim's emotional and mental wellbeing is profound and long-lasting. The constant barrage of undermining and belittling gestures takes an immense toll on the victim's psyche, leaving them feeling emotionally battered and overwhelmed.

Using Body Language to Intimidate:

Symbolic aggression can involve the perpetrator using physical gestures or postures to intimidate, such as standing too close, making threatening gestures, or blocking the victim's exit. These behaviors can induce fear and a sense of helplessness.

Dominating or Controlling Space:

Perpetrators of symbolic aggression may exert control over physical spaces, such as taking over areas the victim claims as their own, locking them out of the house, or using space to intimidate and create dependency. This can make the victim feel trapped, unsafe, or insignificant.

Giving a Gift:

After a victim ends a relationship with a controlling partner, the abuser may send gifts accompanied by a card saying, "Sorry, I love you." They may find where you work or live and send excessive and unwanted gifts. Note these are unwanted and boundary crossing. While this may seem like a reconciliatory gesture to the outside, to the victim it can be perceived as a threatening tactic, implying that the abuser will go to great lengths to manipulate and track their location.

Using Looks and Facial Signals:

Partners in an intimate relationship often have an understanding of each other's non-verbal cues. However, in the context of symbolic aggression, these looks and signals can be used to intimidate, frighten, or assert dominance.

Verbal Intimidation:

Abusers may employ verbal tactics to intimidate and dominate their partners. This can include constantly being in the victim's face, questioning their actions, and demanding attention, leading to feelings of fear and being controlled.

Using Objects and Possessions:

Symbolic aggression may include the display of weapons or damaging possessions that hold value to the victim. Destroying items, hiding important documents, or defacing personal belongings can be used as a form of control and intimidation.

Cyber Abuse:

The invention of the internet and other technologies, creates more nuanced control tactics and opportunities from the covert psychological abuser. Digital voyeurism serves as a manifestation of cyberstalking, wherein abusers exploit various technologies to assert control and dominance over their current or former partners. Within this distressing realm, the abuser intrusively monitors their partner's activities, relentlessly infringing upon their privacy and personal space, even when unwelcome to do so.

The abuser deploys an array of tactics, resorting to creating additional fake accounts to surreptitiously surveil their partner's activities, even in the face of being blocked. In their relentless pursuit of control, they may manipulate others into monitoring their partner on their behalf, effectively extending the reach of their digital surveillance network. Going to extreme lengths, they may stoop to eavesdropping on private conversations through tapping phone lines, installing hidden cameras and listening devices, and breaching their partner's internet banking and other personal accounts.

Moreover, the abuser engages in other forms of cyberstalking, inundating their partner with excessive and unwelcome texts, calls, emails or voice messages, creating an incessant barrage that intrudes upon their emotional boundaries. An invasion of privacy persists as they check through their partner's phones for contacts and messages, feasting upon intimate details to maintain their hold over them. Utilizing GPS and caller ID, they relentlessly track and pursue their partner, transforming technology into a sinister tool of surveillance and control.

The psychological impact of digital voyeurism and cyberstalking is deeply traumatic, leaving the victim feeling as though the abuser is constantly monitoring them. The barrage of surveillance and unwanted contact engenders a sense of powerlessness, causing the victim to question their safety.

Degradation:

Degradation is an especially insidious form of abuse involving behaviors that dehumanize and inflict deep emotional wounds. At its core lies the abuser's campaign to diminish the victim's dignity through derogatory language and even subtle put-downs. This chips away at the victim's self-worth, leaving them vulnerable.

Further, the abuser may deny basic needs and withholds essential resources or support. This is done to undercut the victim's security as their confidence and autonomy erodes.

Examples of Degradation:

One of the most prevalent methods is the use of derogatory language. The abuser employs hurtful terms to belittle the victim, inflicting emotional wounds through derogatory names like "slut" or "whore."

Constant correction serves as another means of control, systematically eroding the victim's confidence by relentlessly criticizing and scrutinizing their actions and statements. However this can also be implications that the victim is unintelligent, unattractive, unimportant, immature, disgusting etc. and can take on more subtle underhanded forms.

Deprivation takes a particularly sinister form as the abuser restricts fundamental necessities, including sleep, food, or healthcare. This calculated manipulation leaves the victim in a state of vulnerability and dependence.

Public humiliation can also contribute to this. The abuser uses public humiliation as a weapon exposing the victim to shame and embarrassment in social settings, further eroding their self-esteem.

Cultural and spiritual ridicule extend the scope of this abuse, as the abuser disparages the victim's cultural traditions, spiritual beliefs, interests, ideas, and desires, erasing their identity.

These forms of degradation, among other tactics result in the suppression of the victim's potential. The abuser's need for control and to maintain a certain image often leads to the slow psychological and spiritual decay.

Jealousy and possessiveness play a destructive role in this cycle, as the abuser resorts to degrading comments and baseless accusations. The abuser may also manufacture jealousy by comparisons to others, whether ex-partners or family members, further intensify the abuse, compelling the victim to alter their identity to meet unfair expectations.

Degradation also includes body shaming and controlling behaviors, such as dictating attire choices, further perpetuating the victim's vulnerability. These may initially come off as preferences, but the abuser will begin to use more overt tactics to indicate how the victim should look and behave.

The abuser exploits the vulnerabilities of their partner to assert dominance and maintain a facade of superiority.

For instance, the victim refrains from achieving personal goals to avoid threatening the abuser's fragile ego. This self-destructive cycle perpetuates the belief that the victim deserves such treatment, despite a deeper awareness that they deserve better.

Over-Protection Disguised As Caring:

Over-protection, cloaked under the guise of caring, presents a deeply concerning aspect within the context of abusive relationships. This pattern encompasses a range of behaviors, with the abuser resorting to tactics such as relentless harassment about imagined affairs, incessant and obsessive possessive jealousy, or resorting to extreme measures such as frequently calling or unexpectedly appearing at the victim's workplace to monitor and scrutinize their every move, all done under the guise of caring and protecting the victim.

At the crux of this over-protection lies a pervading sense of control that the abuser seeks to exert over their partner, leaving them feeling suffocated and smothered. The relentless harassment and questioning becomes a means to instill fear and insecurity in the victim, causing them to constantly second-guess their actions and interactions with others.

Furthermore, the abuser obsessively monitors and scrutinizes the victim's interactions with others, seeking to isolate them from friends and family. This possessiveness becomes an all-consuming force, leaving the victim feeling trapped and cut off from their support network.

In the abuser's relentless pursuit of control, they resort to intrusive tactics, incessantly calling or unexpectedly showing up at the victim's workplace, effectively encroaching upon their personal space and privacy. Such actions cause immense distress and unease, undermining the victim's sense of security and autonomy.

These behaviors form part of a toxic pattern of over-protection that goes beyond genuine care and concern, inflicting emotional harm and eroding the victim's sense of agency and self-worth. The abuser's actions are driven by an insatiable need for dominance and control, leaving the victim feeling emotionally imprisoned and vulnerable.

Inappropriate Restrictions/Monitoring:

This form of psychological abuse manifests through the imposition of inappropriate restrictions by one partner upon the other, constituting a clear violation of fundamental human rights. This form of abuse takes on a troubling dimension, as it involves a series of ongoing behaviors that significantly constrain and limit a person's life, stifling their sense of freedom and autonomy.

Intrusions become a common tactic employed by the abuser, as they invade the victim's personal space and boundaries, effectively denying them the privacy that is essential to a healthy and trusting relationship. Discouragement of personal interests becomes another means of control, as the abuser undermines the victim's passions and pursuits, leaving them feeling invalidated and unimportant.

Monitoring takes on a dimension within the context of psychological abuse, as the abuser obsessively watches and scrutinizes the victim's actions, fostering an environment of constant fear and surveillance. In this atmosphere of control, the victim's individuality is further stifled, as they are systematically denied the space and freedom.

The abuser's inappropriate restrictions extend beyond emotional confines, seeping into the physical realm as well. The victim may find their time outside the house strictly controlled and restricted, leaving them feeling confined and isolated from the outside world.

Denial Minimizing & Blaming:

Denial, minimizing, rationalization, justification, and blaming illustrate how psychological abusers avoid taking responsibility for their actions:

Denial: They deny their controlling behavior and refuse to acknowledge that they have been abusive or caused harm.

Minimizing: They may admit that they have done something harmful but downplay the severity of their behavior and its impact. They might say things like "It wasn't that bad, get over it."

Rationalization: They often rationalize their behavior by providing logical explanations or justifications for their actions. They may try to reason that their controlling behavior was a one-time occurrence or compare their behavior to that of others.

Justification: They shift the blame onto the victim, claiming that their behavior was a direct result of the victim's actions or failure to meet their expectations. For example, they might say, "I wouldn't have behaved this way if you had done what I expected of you.".

Blaming: They admit to using abusive and controlling behaviors but place the blame solely on the victim. They take no ownership or responsibility for their actions. They may blame the victim for their behavior, manipulate the situation to make the victim doubt themselves, or shift attention away from their own actions.

Threats and Emotional Manipulation:

A dynamic that can emerge in abusive relationships involves threats and emotional manipulation. At times, the abusive partner may make chilling threats to harm their partner, children, or other family members. While clearly reprehensible, these threats often arise from a place of desperation and perceived lack of control. The abusive partner resorts to these scare tactics as a misguided attempt to regain dominance in the relationship by instilling profound fear in their partner.

In other cases, the abusive partner may use emotional pleas and manipulation, rather than direct threats. They may say things like, "I'll kill myself if you leave me," exploiting their partner's compassion. While highly concerning, these emotionally manipulative tactics stem from a feeling of vulnerability and fear of abandonment. The abusive partner wrongly uses their partner's empathy against them, trying to coerce them into staying in the relationship. However naive, a small part of the abusive partner likely hopes these overwrought statements will lead to receiving more love and understanding themselves.

Being on the receiving end of threats and emotional manipulation in a relationship can be an immensely difficult and painful experience. The victim is left bearing the brunt of their partner's dysfunctional attempts to maintain control through causing fear, guilt, and obligation.

False Promises:

Another mind game involves insincere promises of change. When the victim gathers the courage to leave, the abusive partner often launches into dramatic proclamations of transformation. They profess a sudden willingness to reform themselves, cease their harmful actions, and become a better partner. The victim understandably wants to believe these promises, clinging to a glimmer of hope that the relationship could improve. They may recall the person they initially fell in love with and long for that version of their partner to return.

This exposes the victim to tremendous disappointment and renewed abuse. In most cases, the abusive partner's promises prove empty, vanishing as soon as the threat of separation passes. The victim is left feeling manipulated and deceived, while the abusive partner resumes the same behaviors as before. While profoundly disillusioning, the victim can use this experience to find clarity that the relationship is irreparable. The abusive partner is responsible for repeatedly making insincere vows, not the victim for daring to hope.

Post-Separation Abuse:

Ending an abusive relationship does not always guarantee safety and freedom from mistreatment. Abusive partners frequently continue controlling and harassing behaviors even post-separation. They may stalk their former partner physically or online, track their movements, or spy on them while letting the victim know that they are doing so to maintain a sense of power. They may also flood their ex-partner with unwelcome gifts, letters, messages, and calls, violating boundaries. The abusive partner feels threatened by loss of access and control and tries to reestablish contact through these coercive means.

Misusing Legal Proceedings:

In some cases, former abusive partners may misuse legal processes like court hearings and filings to continue controlling or harassing their ex. They may file excessive motions or drag out court cases to emotionally and financially drain the other person, rather than resolving issues fairly. This can leave the victim feeling overwhelmed and powerless. Though certainly difficult to deal with, staying calm and working with a good lawyer can help the victim advocate for themselves effectively.

Ex-partners may also perpetrate economic abuse by refusing to pay spousal or child support. By withholding this support, the ex-partner imposes financial instability and stress on the victim and children. This compounds the challenges of transitioning out of the relationship and establishing an independent life. It reflects a troubling attempt by the ex-abuser to maintain control through undermining the victim's financial agency.

Using Social Institutions & Social Prejudices:

The abuser will use various social and legal institutions to exert control over their intimate partners. Examples include:

Using the legal system to stop the victim from moving town or country: They prevent their partners from leaving by filing legal cases and using court proceedings to control their freedom of movement.

Using the legal system to fight for custody of children: The abuser engages in custody battles, not necessarily because they genuinely care about their children, but as a tactic to maintain power and control over their ex-partner. They use their financial resources to manipulate the legal system.

Coercive tactics that lead to the victim getting a criminal record: The abuser provokes situations that result in their partner being arrested or prosecuted for minor offenses, deliberately trying to give them a criminal record.

Using government agencies that provide financial benefits to single parents: The abuser exploits the system by making false accusations or providing misleading information to these agencies to undermine their ex-partner's financial support or benefits.

Using government agencies that manage child support payments: The abuser exploits loopholes in the system to evade or minimize their financial obligations toward supporting their children. They change jobs frequently to avoid having their wages garnished for child support.

Using child protection services to coercively threaten the children's parent: The abuser falsely report child abuse or manipulate child protection services to threaten and intimidate their ex-partner, knowing that such allegations can lead to severe consequences for the children and the parent.

Chapter 5

Narcissistically Organized Relationships

Upon delving into the book's introduction, you may have come across the terms "narcissistic relationship" and "narcissistically organized relationship."

It is essential to emphasize the distinction between a narcissistically *organized* relationship as it does not focus on the abuser rather, it involves objectively examining patterns of personality, behavior and cycles within the relationship that are undeniably present. If you find yourself entangled in these patterns, or witnessing these behaviors, it can indicate being caught in a cycle of abuse within a narcissistically organized relationship also called a narcissistic relationship. Recognizing a narcissistic relationship often involves understanding the dynamics and cycle of idealization, devaluation, and discard stages commonly observed in such relationships.

We will dive deeper and explore how these relationship phases are observed. As an overview, in the initial stages of a relationship, the narcissistic individual clings to an idealized perception, perceiving their partner as flawless and extraordinary. Over time, the idealizations that once adorned the person the narcissistic individual was infatuated with lose their shine. As imperfections become more apparent, the rosy image starts to fadeAs and reality sets the stage for the devaluation phase, the narcissistic individual critically judges their once-adored partner.

Over time, the relationship tends to grow increasingly fraught, often culminating in a painful conclusion where the narcissistic individual becomes cruel, callous or displays a lack of empathy, care or concern for the other partner. It is important to note that these fantasies of ideal love are unrealistic and based on a distorted perception of relationships. In reality, no person can fulfill the narcissistic individual's expectations consistently. So when real relationships fall short of the narcissistic person's fantasy, they may become disappointed, angry, or disillusioned.

Here's a breakdown of these stages and how they display in relationships:

Idealization Stage: In the initial phase of the relationship, the narcissistic partner engages in intense idolization. They shower the other person with excessive admiration, attention, and affection. They may idealize their partner, placing them on a pedestal and making them feel special, valued, and loved. This stage is often characterized by grand gestures, love bombing, and an overwhelming focus on the other person's needs and desires.

Signs during this stage may include:

- Rapid and intense expressions of love and affection.
- Overwhelming attention and flattery.
- Grand gestures or lavish displays of affection.
- Future faking, or early implications of a future together ie. marriage.
- Projection of an idealized image of the relationship or partner.

1. Intense Charm and Flattery: During the idealization phase, a narcissistic abuser will use their charm and charisma to draw you in. They excel at saying all the right things, making you feel like the most important person in their world. Their compliments may feel excessive and too good to be true. They idealize you, creating an image of the perfect partner for them in their mind.

2. Rapid Progression: Narcissistic people are known for their ability to fast-track relationships. They will push for early commitments, such as moving in together, getting engaged, or even talking about marriage and children shortly after meeting. This accelerated pace can feel

exhilarating, as if you've finally found someone who is as invested in the relationship as you are. But be cautious, as this could be a red flag indicating the idealization phase.

3. Love-Bombing: Love-bombing is a key characteristic of the idealization phase. Narcissistic people will bombard you with affection, attention, and gifts. They may constantly send you messages, shower you with compliments, and make grand gestures of love. They want you to believe that you are their perfect match and that they can't live without you. This excessive attention creates a sense of dependency and can make you feel special and desired. During this stage they may employ tactics that manufacture a "soulmate effect". These tactics include future faking and mirroring.

In the early stages of a relationship, a narcissistic abuser may utilize a tactic known as "future faking" to manipulate their partner's emotions and perceptions. For instance, very early into dating, the abuser might say something like:

"I wonder what you would look like in a wedding dress. What type of dress would you wear?" inappropriately early into the relationship.

Comments like these are designed to foster a false sense of emotional intimacy and a future between two people who barely know each other. The abuser is projecting a fictional future in order to hook their partner and elicit premature thoughts of commitment.

While such musings may seem innocently romantic at first, in reality, this "future faking" sets up unrealistic expectations about the relationship very early on. The abuser is using this ploy to create a sense of destiny and to love bomb their partner. These insinuations can include plans for marriage, starting a family, moving in together, or other significant life plans. They may use future faking as a means to maintain control over their partner or to maintain a false sense of harmony and security within the relationship.

In the early stages of dating, mirroring is a manipulation tactic where the narcissistic abuser copies or mimics the victim's interests, traits, habits or hobbies. For example, the victim mentions to their partner that they are into a specific food, game, movie, music etc. The abuser who previously showed no interest in these things, begins professing a sudden deep interest in them.

The abuser may begin to adopt the victim's mannerisms, dressing style, food preferences, experiences and political beliefs. The victim finds themselves taken aback at how the abuser is changing. This may be somewhat obvious to the abuser's friends and family as well but they may not see this as a concern. Narcissistic abusers have an ambiguous sense of self so they find it quite easy to adopt mannerisms, traits and preferences of others.

While it may seem flattering at first, the abuser is simply mirroring the victim as a way to manufacture false compatibility. By reflecting the victim's identity and interests, they ingratiate themselves with the victim more quickly. The mirroring serves to create an illusion that the abuser and victim have an instant bond and creates a premature enmeshment.

4. Placing You on a Pedestal: Narcissistic people see their targets as extensions of themselves, objects to fulfill their needs. During the idealization phase, they will put you on a pedestal, making you believe you are flawless and irreplaceable. They may idealize your qualities, accomplishments, and even your appearance. This pedestal serves as a way to manipulate and control you later in the devaluation phase, as they expect you to live up to their inflated image of you.

5. Love-Bombing versus Authentic Connection: It's crucial to differentiate between genuine love and the love-bombing tactics of a narcissist. True love takes time to develop and grow. The intensity and speed of a narcissist's affection may initially feel exhilarating, but it's important to question whether it's based on a real connection. If they are saying or doing highly inappropriate things that would typically be reserved for much later on in a relationship like professing love or implying marriage within the first three months this can be an indication of "future faking".

While manipulation exists, narcissistic people often do believe they are in love with you at the early stages of the relationship, but their love is based on idealization and their own self-interest. They are infatuated with the image they've created of you, rather than truly knowing and loving you as an individual. This distinction is crucial to understand, as it reveals that their love is conditional and centered around themselves as they cannot truly connect with their intimate partners in healthy ways.

Devaluation Stage: As the relationship progresses, the narcissistic partner begins to devalue their partner. They may become critical, dismissive, or emotionally distant. They begin to undermine their partner's self-esteem, belittle them, and question their worth. This devaluation can take various forms, including verbal and emotional abuse, manipulation, gaslighting, and controlling behaviors. The narcissistic partner may oscillate between moments of extreme praise and devaluation, creating confusion and emotional instability for their partner.

The devaluation phase in a relationship with a narcissistic abuser stems from a stark contrast between their idealized version of you and the real you with flaws. Initially, they treated you amazingly as they created an idealized image of you within their minds. However, as they start noticing imperfections that don't match their ideal, they begin the devaluation process to manipulate you back into that image.

The narcissistic abuser attempts to coerce and mold you, treating you as an "external object," to align you with their internally created idealized representation of you. They introduce an "internal object" that is ideal that represents their version of you. Through abusive tactics, they aim to reshape and sculpt you to perfectly fit into this internal idealized representation, thereby eliminating any dissonance between the real you and their fantasy.

The abuse they inflict serves as a means to control you, molding you to merge and fuse seamlessly with their idealized image of you, effectively eradicating any discrepancies between reality and their perception.

Signs during this stage may include:

- Frequent criticism, insults, or jabs at the target.
- Gaslighting and manipulation to distort the target's perception of reality.
- Emotional and psychological abuse, such as humiliation or withholding affection.
- Sudden shift in affection including withholding affection or intimacy.
- Inconsistent or unpredictable behavior, creating confusion and emotional distress.
- Blaming the target for any issues or problems within the relationship.

Discard or Abandonment Stage: In the discard stage, the narcissistic abuser may withdraw their affection and love without explanation or closure. They may discard the target as if they were disposable, moving on to seek validation and control from new sources. This phase can be emotionally devastating for the target, leaving them feeling discarded, confused, and emotionally shattered.

The "discard" can also take the form of a "reverse discard," wherein the narcissistic abuser creates an unbearably miserable environment, leaving the victim with no choice but to leave. They often use this tactic to portray themselves as the victim, reaching out to their friends and family, claiming they had tried everything, been a good partner, and cannot comprehend why the victim is acting this way.

Despite whether they discarded you or if you left the relationship, signs during this stage may include:

- Sudden withdrawal of affection and emotional support.
- Coldness, indifference, or a complete lack of empathy towards the target.
- Disregard for the target's emotional well-being or needs.
- Pursuing new sources of admiration and validation.
- Possible attempts to devalue and demean the target further during the discard.

Hoovering: While not always present in narcissistically organized relationships, one of the most distressing tactics employed by narcissists is called "hoovering," a term derived from the Hoover vacuum cleaner, symbolizing their relentless efforts to draw their victims back into their lives. Hoovering is a manipulative strategy designed to maintain control over the victim, making it challenging for them to break free from the toxic relationship. This stage is usually placed before the final "discard" but it may also present after being discarded.

Signs during this stage may include:

- Love Bombing and gift-giving
- False promises of change
- Gaslighting and guilt-tripping

But why do we call it Narcissistic Abuse? Abuse is abuse right? And any form can be extremely damaging. However, narcissistic abuse refers to a *specific* type of abuse that occurs in relationships with narcissistic individuals. Narcissistic abuse contains three core elements that set it apart from other types of abuse:

Deception and Manipulation of Identity

At the heart of narcissistic abuse is deception related to the narcissist's identity. Narcissists present a false self to others that can be jarring for partners. This "Dr. Jekyll and Mr. Hyde" persona is an ingrained protective mechanism. Regardless of intent, this deception has devastating impacts on loved ones, leaving them confused, betrayed, and traumatized after seeing both sides of the narcissistic individual. This shift from the kind loving person we are familiar with to a cruel or abusive person devoid of empathy is incredibly jarring. Our minds have difficulty holding those two truths and thus creates cognitive dissonance.

Lack of Empathy and Emotional Invalidation

Another hallmark of narcissistic abuse is a pronounced lack of empathy and emotional invalidation from the narcissist. Minimization, dismissal, and an extreme lack of compassion are common, usually observed within the discard and devaluation phases.

The Idealization-Devaluation-Discard Cycle

Narcissistic relationships follow a cycle of idealization, devaluation, and discard. The narcissist idealizes a partner, then devalues and discards them. They may later "hoover" to restart the cycle. This recurring pattern is specific to narcissistic abuse.

While this cycle occurs subconsciously, it remains highly damaging for victims. The whiplash between idealization and devaluation has severe psychological impacts. In summary, the deception, lack of empathy, and idealization-devaluation cycle make narcissistic abuse a distinct form of abuse when perpetrated by narcissistic individuals. The behaviors can in some cases be unconsciously driven, but still profoundly damaging for victims.

Chapter 6

Stages Of Manipulation

Manipulation, as defined by the Oxford Dictionary, means cleverly controlling or unfairly influencing people or situations. The essence of manipulation is self-serving – it aims to fulfill the manipulator's goals, often at odds with your best interests. Instead of being upfront about their intentions and why they need something from you, manipulators use tactics to persuade or influence you. They often exploit your vulnerabilities, particularly certain emotions.

So, what emotions make us vulnerable to manipulation? Emotions like fear, guilt, shame, obligation, confusion, lowered self-esteem, anxiety, and a sense of not measuring up or feeling "not good enough" can make us susceptible. Manipulators leverage these feelings. They use them as entry points to control our thoughts and actions for their own gain. For instance, if a manipulator knows you're afraid of being alone or abandoned, they'll use that fear to their advantage. They'll push you to do what they want, as you try to avoid feeling those uncomfortable emotions.

This is how manipulation works – it takes advantage of our instinct to avoid feelings that make us uneasy. Manipulators are skilled at exploiting this vulnerability. In a nutshell, manipulation thrives because we naturally want to escape emotions that bring discomfort or make us feel inadequate.

Manipulators have a handful of strategies that they deploy to size you up and determine the most effective approach. Do you respond more to fear or anxiety? Is guilt or obligation your trigger? Perhaps shame, especially if you struggle with a lower sense of self-worth and a desire for self improvement. This collection of tactics is often referred to as F.O.G. Which stands for Fear, Obligation and Guilt.

Manipulation is rarely a single line uttered. It's more of a gradual grooming process where manipulators engage in subtle gaslighting to discern your triggers and vulnerabilities. They employ a variety of maneuvers, not just one phrase, to elicit emotions like fear, guilt, shame, obligation, confusion, lowered self-esteem, anxiety etc.

If the manipulator aims to instill guilt, they might say things like, "You always do this to me." casting themselves as the victim. They'll query, "Why can't you ever let things go?" or suggest that you're being selfish by not complying. Their goal is to make you feel bad about your boundaries or choices, inducing guilt and making you feel responsible for their emotions.

By fostering a sense of guilt, they secure their foothold and proceed with additional tactics and narratives. Gradually, these tactics are repeated in various forms to further their agenda, whether it's persuading you to give something or to lower your boundaries.

Switching gears, when manipulators use fear or foster anxiety in their interactions, they're aware that you are quite dependent on them, often making them a focal point of your life. The relationship has become a lifeline, impacting your ability to self-nurture or love yourself. This kind of fear and dependency becomes their leverage.

If fear is your vulnerability, they might create an environment of anxiety, where you feel like you're walking on eggshells. They may employ threats or use passive-aggressive comments that undermine your self-esteem or abilities, exploiting your insecurities.

Alternatively, manipulators might tap into your areas of shame. They'll focus on what you're sensitive about, aiming to trigger reactions. This could involve blaming you, making comparisons, or subtly undermining your self-confidence. By highlighting these weaknesses, they exert control, reinforcing their authority and influence. To recognize these tactics, you need to ask yourself if someone is trying to put you down, shame you, or exploit your insecurities.

Another group of tactics a manipulator often employs is cunning logical fallacies during arguments. Those fallacies are "appeals to authority", "red herrings", ad hominem", "circular reasoning" and the "straw man" fallacy. First, the appeal to authority fallacy. Imagine someone declaring their opinion as gospel because they're supposedly an expert. They wield their self-proclaimed authority as the ultimate truth, thereby invalidating other perspectives. Victims struggle to defend themselves due to feelings of inadequacy, especially if they lack equivalent experience, expertise, or credentials.

Now, let's delve into the intricacies of the red herring fallacy. Here, the manipulator adeptly sidesteps accountability by steering the discourse towards a different, unrelated subject. This maneuver serves as a smokescreen, effectively diverting attention away from their own actions. As a result, victims become ensnared in dialogues that veer off course from the core matter at hand. This deliberate distraction not only disrupts the original focus but also undermines attempts at defense, as the spotlight is redirected onto the new topic. In essence, the red herring fallacy is a skillful tactic that capitalizes on the art of deflection, rendering it challenging for victims to navigate and reclaim the discussion's intended direction.

Next, the ad hominem fallacy. In moments when your emotions take a backseat as your partner persistently prioritizes their needs over yours, an unsettling dynamic unfolds. When you voice your hurt, they casually brand you as sensitive, trivializing the depth of your emotions. This fallacy entails an offensive against your character rather than a direct engagement with the current matter. As a result, victims find themselves stumbling, feeling a personal affront and disoriented by the sudden pivot of attention away from the real concern.

Enter the circular reasoning fallacy. Here, the manipulator asserts their unwavering correctness, using their self-proclaimed intellectual prowess as a foundation. This creates a self-reinforcing loop of logic that lacks any substantiating evidence or reasoning. Victims encounter an uphill struggle to provide a rebuttal, as the manipulator cleverly presents their stance as impervious to challenge, leaving no space for opposing viewpoints to gain traction.

Lastly, let's discuss the straw man fallacy. This is when someone distorts what you're saying to make it easier for them to attack. Instead of addressing your real argument, they create a simplified and twisted version of it. By attacking this distorted version, they try to make you appear wrong or unreliable. In simple terms, the straw man fallacy involves misrepresenting your point so they can knock down a weaker version of it. This tactic is used to deceive and divert attention from the main issue.

Manipulation in relationships can be incredibly damaging, but it often happens gradually through a series of relationship progression strategies meant to hook you into the cycle and prime you for manipulation. The opening act of manipulation within a relationship is known as love bombing, which includes an extravagant display of affection and attention that envelops the victim. It's a torrent of emotion that leaves them feeling as though they've discovered their soulmate, their long-sought dream person. In this intoxicating whirlwind, the victim is bathed in a radiant light of recognition and appreciation, becoming a cherished object of desire.

Once you are emotionally hooked, the next stage is devaluation. The manipulator suddenly withdraws the affection and attention. This leaves the victim feeling worthless, destabilized, and craving the love bombing again. When the victim questions this sudden withdrawal, the manipulator turns to gaslighting. This involves outright denying conversations or events, minimizing concerns, or blatantly distorting the truth to sow seeds of doubt in the victim's mind. The manipulator is so adamant on their reality that the victim begins to believe the manipulator as well. They start questioning their own reality.

In an effort to win back the manipulator's approval, and affection they once basked in, the victim's identity enters a phase of submission. Whereby they increasingly submit to the manipulator's version of reality and dismiss their own needs and instincts. They contort their own beliefs and suppress their instincts, surrendering to the manipulator's version of reality. The victim continually attempts to please the manipulator.

This way a manipulator molds your behavior is through a technique called "entraining". Entraining refers to a conditioning technique manipulators use in an attempt to influence others' behavior. It involves using repetitive actions and words to try to reinforce desired conduct and discourage unwanted conduct.

For example, someone may use subtle gestures like scoffing or repeatedly criticizing the same issue to indicate disapproval. They may also use more overt verbal attacks, followed by giving gifts or affection as a reward when the desired behavior is displayed.

It's very similar to the classical conditioning exemplified by Pavlov's experiments with dogs. The goal is to shape the victim's actions through a pattern of punishment and reward. This technique of conditioning behavior is sometimes employed by those with narcissistic traits to maintain control in their relationships.

After enduring cycles of love bombing, devaluation, and gaslighting, the victim begins experiencing a loss of self. They lose touch with who they are as a person and increasingly believe the negative image of themselves portrayed by the manipulator.

At this point, the relationship has damaged the victim's self-esteem and identity. But they have become emotionally addicted to their manipulative partner. They crave the emotional highs of those intermittent love bombing episodes, leading them to repeatedly reconcile. Many controlling, toxic people employ masterful manipulation tactics to hook, confuse, and control their partners.

Manipulators use these techniques strategically, like following a playbook. The more familiar you are with their tactics, the quicker you can detect them and avoid getting drawn in.

Pay close attention to any sudden major shifts in their communication patterns, affection, treatment of you, or declarations about the relationship. Drastic changes are huge red flags. For example, if your partner suddenly goes from acting loving and attentive to withdrawing and disinterested, take note. Don't let yourself become emotionally addicted or hooked too quickly when dating someone new. Give relationships time to unfold naturally to reveal any red flags. Rushing into intense intimacy and commitment too fast is a sign of manipulation.

Maintain your own perspective and sense of reality. Don't automatically believe whatever you're being told or allow your version of events to be distorted. Trust your own instincts, memories, and experiences. If you catch someone lying or trying to confuse you, speak up and name what's happening. Refuse to internalize the abuser's put-downs to appease them once you see manipulation tactics surfacing. You don't deserve mistreatment. Don't accept excuses or apologies without changed behavior.

Reaffirm your worth and who you are as a person. Don't lose your identity in someone else's distorted narrative about you. Stay grounded in your core self. Prioritize your emotional, psychological and physical safety. Don't tolerate mistreatment hoping you can "fix" the relationship. Invest in strong personal boundaries, confidence, and self-love. Surround yourself with people who show you authentic care, respect and understanding. You deserve healthy relationships free of manipulation.

Chapter 7

The Silent Assassin: Examples of Verbal Abuse Beyond Shouting & Unveiling the Subtle Forms of Harm

"Being quietly observant, judgmental and showing gestures of superiority are characteristics you'll find in a covert narcissist. They tend to do this with an air of smugness, which can leave you feeling belittled, confused and often like you're simply not good enough."

– Louisa Cox

Verbal abuse is often associated with loud and aggressive outbursts, but it's important to recognize that abuse can manifest in more subtle and insidious ways. We all know the stereotype of abusive men and women as being these angry violent people but a common tactic for covert abusers is calmness. They have two realities: the internal reality of anger and contempt and the external facade of calmness. And because they're calm, it blinds us to their covert abuse tactics. The abuse is hidden under a calm composed facade. They do this in order to psychologically manipulate you into believing that their behavior is not the problem but rather it's your reaction that's the issue. In this chapter, we will explore the world of covert abusers and shed light on how an abusive person doesn't need to resort to yelling or screaming to inflict emotional harm.

The primary objective of an abuser is to establish control over others in order to fulfill their needs, wants, preferences etc. They employ various tactics, including skillful manipulation, subtle insults, and gradually eroding the victim's self-confidence. It can be challenging to recognize their controlling agenda when they don't resort to name-calling or physical violence. However, some of the most controlling abusers refrain from using derogatory language or engaging in physical aggression. This can lead the victim to believe that they are in a functional relationship, as the typical signs of obvious dysfunction are not present.

In the complex realm of narcissistically organized relationships, interactions with toxic individuals can take various forms. While many have encountered explosive outbursts of rage, characterized by yelling and screaming, others have experienced a more subtle and covert type of aggression.

Narcissistic rage can be terrifying. It can be hot or cold. There are two types of rage usually present in narcissistic relationships. The hot rag where they blow up and spew verbal assaults and cold rage. A person displaying cold rage may employ the silent seething or the silent treatment which is a form of emotional abuse, involving the calculated use of silence and withdrawal as tools for punishment and manipulation. The covert abuser employs tactics such as passive-aggressive comments, sulking, ignoring, and stonewalling, silent treatment and cold indifference to induce confusion and frustration in their victims.

Verbal abuse is not limited to yelling or screaming. It is essential to challenge the prevailing belief that abuse can only be recognized when it is accompanied by loud and aggressive behavior. The absence of shouting does not diminish the harmful effects of verbal abuse. By broadening our understanding, we can identify the various tactics used by abusers to manipulate and control their victims. Verbal abuse is a destructive form of mistreatment that extends beyond the misconception that it must involve shouting or screaming.

Negging:

Covert abusers use a tactic called "negging" as a form of emotional manipulation. The goal of negging is to undermine a victim's self-confidence through backhanded compliments or subtle insults. For example, an abusive partner might say "Wow, you look so pretty when you actually put on makeup", "You look much nicer this morning" or "Your friends are in such great shape! You should workout with them." Another negging tactic is criticizing someone's interests or tastes, like "Really, you like that music? Yeah I just don't get how you like that type of music." The underlying message of these negging statements is intended to make the recipient feel inadequate, so they will seek validation from the negger. While negging may seem minor at first, being subjected to constant criticism, judgment, and trivialization can gradually undermine a person's self-worth over time. True caring partners build each other up rather than resorting to unhealthy manipulation tactics. There are always kinder ways to share constructive feedback in a relationship.

Belittling:

Belittling is a common tactic used by covert abusers to erode their victims' self-esteem and sense of worth. Through subtle remarks, sarcasm, and condescending tones, abusers aim to make their victims feel small and insignificant. Examples include:

- "You're always so useless. Can't you do anything right?"

- "Wow you're really playing up the whole dumb blonde thing, hu?"

Gaslighting:

Gaslighting is a manipulative technique employed by covert abusers to distort the victim's perception of reality, making them doubt their memory, sanity, and judgment. Examples include:

- "I never said that. You must have misunderstood."

- "You're overreacting. It didn't happen like that at all."

- "I was just joking when I said that."

Backhanded Compliments:

Covert abusers often use backhanded compliments as a means to subtly criticize and demean their victims while maintaining a facade of sincerity. Examples include:

- "You're pretty for someone your size."

- "You know, everyone else may think it's ugly but I love your big nose."

- "Wow, you woke up looking nicer this morning."

- "I love how confident you are, even though you're not very talented."

Withholding Validation:

Covert abusers may withhold love, validation, and emotional support to exert control and instill a sense of dependency in their victims. Examples include:

- Ignoring the victim's achievements and dismissing their accomplishments.

- Refraining from complimenting when you've put obvious effort in your appearance, especially so if you feel good about yourself.

- Rejecting you. This includes rejecting to hug, kiss , hold your hand etc.

Sarcasm and Veiled Insults:

Covert abusers often employ sarcasm and mockery to subtly demean and ridicule their victims. Examples include:

- "Oh, congratulations on your brilliant idea. I'm sure the world is waiting for your genius."

- "You're so funny. I never knew incompetence could be so entertaining."

Verbal abuse goes beyond raised voices, encompassing covert tactics that can inflict deep emotional wounds. By challenging the prevailing belief that abuse must be loud and aggressive, we broaden our understanding and empower individuals to recognize the insidious nature of verbal abuse. Examples such as belittling, gaslighting, backhanded compliments, emotional withholding, sarcasm, and mockery illustrate the covert tactics employed by abusers. It is crucial to raise awareness, support victims, and foster a society that rejects all forms of verbal abuse, whether they are loud or hidden in subtle manipulation.

Covert verbal abuse is designed to undermine a person's self-esteem, causing them to doubt their own worth. Abusers use subtle tactics to chip away at their victims' confidence, such as belittling remarks, condescending tones, and veiled insults. Over time, these subtle messages penetrate the victim's psyche, leaving them with a diminished sense of self and feelings of inadequacy. The absence of shouting does not equate to a lack of verbal abuse.

Chapter 8

Tipping Points: Patterns of Abuse During Key Relationship Milestones

Within the context of abusive relationships, certain pivotal moments can become tipping points that trigger increased instances of abusive behavior. This chapter delves into the patterns of abuse that may emerge when couples move in together, get married, or have a baby, shedding light on the dynamics at play during these significant relationship milestones.

Often, as is typical with a person who has abusive and toxic personalities, they will begin the cycle of abuse when they feel their partner is suitably "hooked". In the initial stages, the relationship may exude a honeymoon-like aura, filled with excitement and passion. However, as time elapses, an undercurrent of tension begins to build, laying the groundwork for the abuser to enact their manipulative and harmful tactics.

Cohabitation can create a shift in dynamics within a relationship. Milestones like moving in together can be significant in a relationship, bringing couples closer and providing opportunities for deeper intimacy. However, in the context of an abusive relationship, it can be a turning point where abusive behaviors become more apparent.

There are several reasons why this might occur:

Intensified Power Imbalance: The cohabitation phase of a relationship, while often seen as a natural progression, can unveil a complex interplay of power dynamics that may significantly impact the emotional landscape of the couple. Within this context, abusers may seize the opportunity to exploit control tactics, further reinforcing their dominance and seeking to erode the victim's sense of autonomy and independence. As the couple takes the significant step of sharing a living space, the dynamics may shift, laying the groundwork for potential abuses of power that threaten the emotional well-being of the victim.

In the cohabitation setting, the abuser may strategically utilize a range of control tactics, manipulating situations and interactions to consolidate their power over the victim. In the early stages covert manipulation takes various forms, from asserting dominance in decision-making to undermining the victim's choices and independence. By establishing a semblance of control within the shared living space, the abuser seeks to create an environment wherein the victim's agency is systematically eroded, making them more susceptible to manipulation and coercion.

As the victim finds themselves in closer proximity to the abuser due to cohabitation, their emotional vulnerabilities become more apparent, providing fertile ground for the abuser to exploit and exert further control. The increasing proximity fosters an environment where the abuser's manipulation may intensify, strategically leveraging emotional vulnerabilities to further cement their dominance and control over the victim's emotional state.

Moreover, the victim's emotional and psychological wellbeing may suffer as a result of the heightened power imbalances that emerge during cohabitation. The sense of vulnerability, coupled with the abuser's strategic manipulation, places the victim at increased risk of falling prey to coercion and psychological abuse.

Escalation of Tension and Stress: The decision to live together marks a significant milestone in any relationship, signifying a deeper commitment and shared journey. However, this cohabitation phase can also unveil a host of new stressors and conflicts, presenting both partners with unique challenges to navigate. Unfortunately, within the context of an abusive relationship, the abuser may view these stressors as opportune moments to intensify their abusive behavior, leveraging them as a means to wield control and assert dominance over the victim. As moments of tension or disagreements arise, the abuser cunningly exploits these vulnerabilities to manipulate and intimidate their partner, further entrenching their hold on the relationship.

During the cohabitation phase, the abuser may systematically exploit the new stressors that naturally arise from shared living arrangements. These stressors could encompass financial responsibilities, division of household chores, or differences in lifestyle preferences. Rather than engaging in open communication and collaborative problem-solving, the abuser seizes these moments as openings to flex their manipulative tactics, seeking to undermine the victim's confidence and exert power.

Disagreements, which are inevitable in any relationship, become potential triggers for the abuser to escalate their abusive behavior. They may adeptly twist these disagreements to their advantage, using gaslighting techniques to make the victim doubt their perceptions or experiences. The abuser may employ various tactics of emotional manipulation, such as guilt-tripping, blame-shifting, or emotional blackmail, to subjugate their partner and maintain control over the narrative.

Stress and Change: Major life transitions have the potential to usher in significant stress and upheaval within a relationship, presenting both partners with a myriad of challenges to navigate. For abusers, these changes can prove particularly difficult to cope with, serving as triggers for the escalation of their abusive behaviors. In the face of these transitions, the abuser may resort to abuse as a misguided attempt to manage their own anxieties and frustrations stemming from the unfamiliar circumstances.

During moments of significant change, such as moving to a new living situation, commitments like marriage or adjusting to parenthood, the abuser may find themselves grappling with heightened levels of uncertainty and insecurity. The unfamiliarity of the new circumstances may amplify their preexisting feelings of inadequacy or fear of losing control. As a result, they may feel compelled to exert dominance over their partner as a means of compensating for their own perceived vulnerabilities.

In their desperate bid to regain a sense of control, the abuser may resort to abusive behaviors as a coping mechanism, seeking solace in the illusion of power they derive from exerting dominance and control over their partner. The abuse serves as a misguided outlet for their internal turmoil and frustration, as they take out frustrations by inflicting harm on their partner to alleviate their own emotional distress.

Additionally, major life transitions can disrupt the established power dynamics within the relationship, leading the abuser to feel threatened or challenged by the changing circumstances. As their control slips away amidst the changes, they may lash out as a means of reasserting their dominance and regaining a semblance of power.

Increased Intimacy and Dependency: The decision to cohabit represents a significant step in any relationship, fostering a deeper level of emotional and physical intimacy between partners. This heightened closeness, while fostering an environment of love and trust in healthy relationships, can, unfortunately, become a double-edged sword in the context of an abusive dynamic. For an abusive individual, the increased proximity and emotional connection that accompany living together provide fertile ground for the exertion of control over their partner. In this intricate web of intimacy, the abuser cunningly exploits the natural dependency and vulnerability that can arise from sharing a living space, leveraging it as a potent means to assert power and dominance.

The closeness resulting from cohabitation can create a sense of emotional interconnectedness, wherein the partners share their lives, aspirations, and vulnerabilities

In healthy relationships, this sense of intimacy fosters a mutual support system, deepening the emotional bond between partners. However, for the abusive individual, the increased emotional and physical proximity affords them unprecedented access to the inner workings of their partner's thoughts and feelings, enabling them to identify and exploit areas of vulnerability.

The dependency that can emerge in cohabiting couples may arise from the shared responsibilities, financial commitments, and intertwined lives. The abuser, recognizing this dependence, may cunningly manipulate it to their advantage. By cultivating an environment where their partner feels reliant on them for various aspects of their daily lives, the abuser gains a foothold to exert control and dominance.

The vulnerabilities that surface in the shared living space can manifest in myriad ways. Emotional vulnerabilities, past traumas, and insecurities may come to the fore when partners live together, providing the abuser with ample opportunities to exploit these sensitive areas for their gain. Whether it be through emotional manipulation, gaslighting, or belittling, the abuser systematically chips away at their partner's self-esteem, leaving them emotionally compromised and increasingly dependent on the abuser's validation.

Sense of Ownership: The advent of significant relationship milestones, such as moving in together, getting married, or sharing the experience of parenthood, can have multifaceted implications on the dynamics between partners. In certain cases, these pivotal moments may inadvertently foster a distorted sense of ownership or entitlement within the mind of the abuser. As a couple embarks on the journey of living together, the abuser may subconsciously begin to perceive the shared living space as their exclusive territory, thereby cultivating a sense of entitlement that emboldens them to exert control and dominance over their partner within that intimate domain.

The concept of ownership, when intertwined with an abusive mindset, engenders a perilous dynamic that undermines the very essence of a healthy, equal partnership. As the couple merges their lives and possessions, the abuser may harbor a misguided belief that the shared space is an extension of themselves, thus conferring them with the right to wield authority and dominance within its confines. This distorted perception leads the abuser to manifest possessive behaviors, viewing their partner as an object or possession to be controlled and manipulated at will.

In this paradigm, the abuser may subtly begin to stake claim over various aspects of the shared living space, seeking to assert their presence and dominance over their partner. Their actions may range from meticulously organizing and controlling the arrangement of items to imposing strict rules and guidelines, effectively diminishing the victim's autonomy within their own home. The abuser may even go so far as to invade the victim's personal space, treating their partner's belongings as an extension of their own, further perpetuating the illusion of ownership.

As the distorted sense of entitlement takes root, the abuser may increasingly infringe upon the victim's personal boundaries, eroding their sense of agency and independence. The shared living space, which should ideally foster an atmosphere of mutual respect and cooperation, becomes tainted by the abuser's controlling and strict adherence to their rules and preferences, creating an environment of emotional coercion and control.

Isolation from Support Networks: Moving in together can sometimes result in the distancing of the abused person from their support networks, such as friends and family. This isolation can make it more challenging for the victim to seek help or escape the abusive situation, as the abuser may exert control over who the victim can interact with or restrict their social connections.

Additionally, pregnancy and marriage can bring about a sense of increased commitment and entanglement in the relationship. Abusive individuals may perceive these events as opportunities to exert greater control over their partner. They may exploit societal expectations around marriage and parenthood to further manipulate and dominate their partner.

Pregnancy and marriage signify significant life changes and increased vulnerability for the victim. Abusers often seek to exert power and control over their partners, and these milestones can be seen as opportunities for them to further assert dominance.

Pregnancy in particular can create a sense of increased dependence on the abuser. The victim may feel a greater need for support and stability during this time, and the abuser may exploit this vulnerability.

Unlike you and I, some abusers view pregnancy as a threat to their control or attention. They may become jealous or feel the need to compete for attention or affection from their partner. This can lead to increased abusive behaviors as they attempt to regain a sense of control and dominance within the relationship.

This behavior is rooted in the inherent traits of narcissistic abusers. Their insatiable need for attention and admiration drives them to become intensely jealous when they perceive any focus or adoration directed elsewhere. This jealousy is not limited to their partners but can extend even to their own children. As their sense of entitlement and ego swells, the abuser demands constant attention, positioning themselves as the center of the universe.

So, when children are born into the equation, the abuser's delusional expectation of undivided attention clashes with the reality that the spotlight cannot always be exclusively on them. This reality check triggers an escalation in their demanding and difficult behavior. The narcissistic mindset perceives love as a limited commodity that they must monopolize. The presence of others in their partner's life, even their own children, is seen as a threat to their perceived supremacy. This deep-seated insecurity and fear of abandonment fuel their insatiable hunger for attention, leading to manipulative and possessive behavior.

Lastly, abusers may intensify their abusive behaviors when their partner is sick, ill or in a vulnerable state. Illness can make individuals feel vulnerable and reliant on others for support and care. Abusers may exploit this vulnerability to assert power and control over their partner. They may use the illness as an opportunity to further dominate and manipulate their partner's choices, actions, and access to resources.

Illness or vulnerability can shift the focus of attention and control away from the abuser, leading to feelings of resentment or jealousy. Some abusers may feel threatened by the attention and care the victim receives during their illness and may seek to regain control by intensifying abusive behaviors.

As you can see, a common theme here and in all abusive dynamics is power and control.

Chapter 9

Frogs In Boiling Water

"One day you will tell your story of how you overcame what you went through and it will be someone else's survival guide."
– Brene Brown

In this chapter, we will explore the dynamics of covert abuse and devaluation and how they present in real-life scenarios. I'll be sharing other survivor's stories including a recounting of my own at the end of this chapter. After each story I'll highlight and explain the instances of covert abuse displayed in each of these stories. As you read through, see how many of these you can spot, considering the knowledge you've acquired about covert abuse and narcissistic relationships throughout this book.

This exercise can be something you can perform after reading each of these accounts. By delving into these stories, I hope you will gain critical insights into how covert abuse can quietly manifest and permeate. My goal is to provide you with a nuanced understanding of the many forms covert and narcissistic abuse can take, revealing the intricate ways power and control dynamics can organically weave themselves into the fabric of a relationship.

Each story will act as a mirror, allowing you to reflect on your own relationship and empowering you to discern these harmful patterns within your own life. I hope that by illuminating these real-life instances, you will be better equipped to identify and comprehend the warning signs and red flags. Knowledge, after all, is power.

The metaphor of placing a frog in boiling water and turning up the heat slowly is often used to describe psychological and covert forms of abuse due to its gradual and insidious nature. Just as the frog may not notice the gradual increase in temperature until it's too late, victims of abuse often find themselves trapped in a toxic dynamic before fully realizing the extent of the damage. After the relationship they may also experience "delayed realization" a phenomena where the victim fails to recognize the severity of the abusive relationship until far after it's ended.

At the beginning of a relationship with a narcissistic abuser, everything may seem idyllic. The narcissistic abuser typically puts on a charming and charismatic façade, idealizing their partner and showering them with attention and affection. This initial phase, known as the love bombing or idealization stage, hooks the victim emotionally, creating a strong bond and attachment.

However, as time goes on, the narcissistic abuser may begin to criticize, control, and demean their partner, using tactics such as gaslighting, manipulation, and verbal or psychological abuse. This transition from idealization to devaluation is akin to turning up the heat on the frog slowly, gradually exposing them to an increasingly hostile environment.

The process of psychological abuse is incremental, making it difficult for the victim to recognize the toxicity until it becomes overwhelming. The narcissistic abuser strategically employs a variety of tactics to chip away at the victim's self-esteem, confidence, and sense of reality. By undermining their perception of themselves and distorting their view of the relationship, the narcissistic abuser gains power and control over their victim.

Much like the frog in boiling water, the victim of psychological abuse may adapt to the escalating mistreatment, rationalizing and making excuses for their behavior. The slow progression of abuse creates a sense of cognitive dissonance, where the victim's perception of the initial love and affection clashes with the growing mistreatment they experience. This cognitive dissonance can keep the victim trapped in the cycle of abuse, hoping that the narcissistic abuser will return to their initial loving state.

The metaphor also highlights the difficulty of escaping covertly abusive relationships. Just as the frog may struggle to jump out of the boiling water once it realizes the danger, victims of covert abuse often face significant obstacles when attempting to leave the relationship. The gradual erosion of their self-esteem, coupled with the narcissistic abuser's manipulative tactics, can leave the victim feeling trapped, helpless, and fearful of the consequences of leaving.

Sofia:

"I would outburst at him and whenever I did he was calm, almost smiling. He seemed to enjoy my eruptions and loss of control of myself. Any emotion I expressed he would tell me that I was deregulating."

My ex husband was a psychologist. He did so many things that were abusive and manipulative but not yelling or name calling so it didn't register as abuse because I believed he knew what was best. For example, we were on our way back home from a bbq party with his doctoral friends. He said "do you realize that you are really awkward in social settings?" I've never thought about that and never heard anyone say that to me. He said that he notices people fake laughing at funny stories I was sharing. He also said he observed people getting bored with my conversation topics. He said that he was only trying to help by pointing out something I was unaware of. He said that it's because people just don't like me much and they are just being polite to me. I would get so confused. These comments would nag at the back of my brain as I did dishes or took care of the kids. I would ruminate over it.

Every time I would push back about the comments he made about me he would say that I don't want to grow and learn. He would tell me that I simply can't observe myself objectively because I lacked awareness and that he knew better than me about who I was because he was a psychologist.

He would constantly undermine my intelligence. During another instance while I was playing tic-tack-toe with our 4yr old she beat me and I started laughing, partly at myself and in surprise at her cleverness. My ex did not laugh, he just raised his eyebrows and said "wow it's actually scary. It shows that you lack future planning and strategic thinking skills".

He began to say that I wasn't good at planning out the day for the children, and so he wrote me a schedule on a whiteboard and told me to follow it. As much as I argued with him about how I had to be flexible because the day just didn't need to be that planned out he insisted. If I deviated from this schedule he would refer to the whiteboard. He would calmly refer to the whiteboard and ask if I was able to read it. He made me feel like a child.

I was so angry and harbored so much resentment. But I was so tired. I would outburst at him and whenever I did he was calm, almost smiling. He seemed to enjoy my eruptions and loss of control of myself. Any emotion I expressed he would tell me that I was deregulating. I would beg him for any empathy. Through my tears he would simply look at me and tell me I was deregulating and that I needed to calm down. He always cushioned his remarks by telling me how concerned he was for me and that he cared about me. He had me convinced that I was the one with the issues and after six years of this insidious marriage I was convinced that I was the one with all the problems. I felt like I was losing my mind.

—

The story above paints a chilling portrait of a relationship characterized by abuse and manipulation, where the abuser's calculated tactics corroded the victim's sense of self and agency. The abuser, who held a professional role as a psychologist, exploited his knowledge and authority to insidiously degrade and control his partner. The manipulation began with subtle yet devastating remarks that targeted the victim's self-esteem. By couching hurtful criticism as well-meaning observations, he skillfully obscured his true intent. This devaluation tactic left the victim emotionally disoriented and questioning her own worth. The abuser's expertise allowed him to cast his assessments as irrefutable truths, leaving the victim trapped in a cycle of self-doubt.

Gaslighting, a hallmark of manipulation, found its insidious place in this narrative. The abuser strategically exploited his professional position to undermine the victim's perception of reality. By portraying himself as the ultimate authority on her emotions and behavior, he systematically dismantled her trust in her own judgment. His claims that she lacked awareness and objectivity effectively silenced her attempts to challenge his narratives. This eroded her autonomy and left her reliant on his version of reality, a reality meticulously shaped to suit his purposes.

Furthermore, the abuser employed isolation and infantilization to amplify his control. From dictating a rigid schedule to belittling her intelligence, he systematically dismantled her independence. His calculated efforts to portray her as incapable and inept reinforced her dependency on him, rendering her more susceptible to his manipulation. The emotional rollercoaster of sporadic affection, mixed with calculated degradation, maintained a grip on her emotions, making it difficult for her to break free from the cycle.

This story is a stark reminder that abuse and manipulation often manifest in ways that extend far beyond overt aggression. The abuser's cunning exploitation of psychological vulnerabilities and professional authority showcases the insidious nature of such relationships. It underlines the importance of recognizing the signs of abuse, even when they are cloaked in seemingly caring gestures or veiled expertise.

<u>Becky:</u>
"I was so far dissociated from my own self and reality, constantly"

I endured two decades of covert abuse in a relationship with a narcissistic abuser. Emotionally beaten down, I lived in denial for years, trapped in a fog of dissociation due to the psychological torment. My boundaries eroded over time, making it impossible for me to express my feelings without facing blame. I believed my partner was superior to me and considered myself lucky to have him; my abuser reinforced that belief.

Skillfully portraying himself as a victim, my partner manipulated me into compliance. Attempts to set boundaries were met with temporary agreement, followed by silent punishment, the cold shoulder, and stonewalling. He would chip away at my defenses until they crumbled. I tried to ignore his habitual flirtations with other women, which he would do in front of me often, aided by his convincing denials of even doing so. He engaged in emotional affairs, but when confronted, he insisted that they were mere friendships, exacerbating my insecurities.

Observing my husband's increasing closeness with a coworker named Mary fueled my suspicions. He spent more time with Mary, laughed freely with her, and even planned joint projects. Despite my discomfort, I felt powerless to confront him due to his gaslighting tactics. Confrontations with my partner over his behavior only led to me being labeled delusional.

My creative YouTube business became a battleground, with my partner slowly taking control of my projects through Mary's assistance. My attempts to assert myself were met with subtle mockery, put downs, and accusations of jealousy. My self-confidence dwindled, and I found myself manipulated into accepting Mary's involvement in my creative endeavors. After months of gaslighting and manipulation, my husband finally confessed his feelings for Mary.

My world crumbled as I learned of my partner's affair with Mary. The manipulation, gaslighting, and cognitive dissonance had taken their toll. Eventually, I found myself engulfed in sexual coercion, my partner using my desire to please him and to rebuild the marriage for his gratification. I was coerced into engaging in his sexual fantasies that I was uncomfortable with.

Despite a period of hope during couples therapy, where my partner presented himself as remorseful, the truth was stark: I understood that he had been using me for his own pleasure, while my identity faded. My abuser then began manipulating the therapist. "They'd tell me to give in to him a little if I'm going to make our marriage work.

He had started therapy as well, so I had some weird kind of hope. And at this point, I wanted to see all the things he had been hiding for years. I needed to see my truth. He and his therapist diagnosed me with borderline personality disorder."

I later went to therapy on my own and realized the depth of the abuse, and with the help of therapy, began to see through the manipulations. Seeking professional help, I consulted a psychiatrist who diagnosed me with CPTSD, chronic depression, and comorbid ADHD. This diagnosis shed light on the complex layers of my mental and emotional struggles.

Over time, I found the strength to detach myself from the toxic relationship and embark on a journey of healing and self-discovery.

— -----

This narrative delves into Becky's journey, revealing her persistent state of bewilderment within the confines of the relationship. Her tormentor not only engaged in triangulation with Mary but also skillfully employed gaslighting and manipulation to implant the belief that no affair was underway.

This manipulation extended to the therapist during the couple's counseling sessions. We like to think that trained professionals are immune to the manipulations of a narcissistic abuser. However, the truth is that many narcissistic abusers can and very often and regularly do manipulate skilled therapists. This can be a shocking and deeply troubling realization. According to professionals like Shahida Arabi, MA *"Manipulative abusers will often put on a charming facade for the therapist, fooling them into thinking they are the true victims. Narcissists will use therapy as a site for further gaslighting their victims, if they even attend at all."*

Which is why I often advocate to my clients and fellow survivors to avoid entering couples counseling when dealing with an adept manipulator and narcissistic abuser.

Ruth

"He stared back blankly and said, "You have two other holes I can use."

After my son was born, I endured years of recurring yeast infections and UTIs that left me miserable most days. Yet I was still expected to be sexually available to my husband whenever he wanted. Only his needs mattered. One time when I had a particularly bad UTI with blood in my urine, I hesitantly asked if we could take a night off from sex given how much pain I was in. He stared back blankly and said, "You have two other holes I can use."

In that moment, it became painfully clear just how little I truly meant to him as a human being. But he had convinced me that his cruelty was love, so I stayed. I was three weeks postpartum when this next encounter occurred. I had just gotten out of the shower and stood nude in front of the mirror, assessing my post-pregnancy body. My husband walked in, looked me up and down, and asked what the scale said. 116 pounds, I replied meekly. He smirked and responded, "Let me know when it says 110." At 5'6, I was already slender.

Throughout our relationship, he would make subtle digs at my looks intended to chip away at my self-esteem and keep me small. Once, he point blank asked if I had ever considered plastic surgery. Taken aback, I said no and asked why. He remarked that my nose was rather bulbous. It never bothered me before, but his words implanted themselves in my psyche, echoing for two decades since.

They know how to say these things in a way that embeds itself like shrapnel. My husband refused to compliment me to teach me a lesson in neediness. We were headed to a Christmas party, and I had on a new dress, did my hair just so, and painted my lips red. When he didn't acknowledge my efforts, I foolishly fished for a compliment, asking if he liked my dress. His eyes went dark, his face twisted in disgust. "What is wrong with you? It's like you need the compliments. It shows your weakness," he seethed. I was crestfallen but dared not show it. I didn't want him lecturing me for "allowing" him to hurt my feelings. He loved to say, "I can't hurt your feelings without your permission." Yet I always had to tiptoe around his feelings. Mine only mattered when it made him look good to others.

—

In Ruth's account, we see a disturbing pattern of covert abuse that encompasses emotional manipulation, sexual coercion, and body-shaming. The abuser in this narrative uses various tactics to control and demean his partner, exploiting her vulnerabilities and eroding her self-esteem.

One of the most disgusting aspects of this abuse is the complete disregard for her physical and emotional well-being. Despite struggling with recurrent yeast infections and UTIs that left her in constant pain and discomfort, Ruth was expected to fulfill her husband's sexual desires without any consideration for her own pain. The dismissive and degrading comment about "having two other holes" serves as a stark example of how the abuser objectified and dehumanized his partner, reducing her an instrument of his pleasure.

Furthermore, her husband used body-shaming as a means of control, making derogatory remarks about her appearance and weight, even when she was already slender. These cruel comments about her body and the suggestion of plastic surgery not only wounded her self-esteem but also left lasting scars on her self-image.

The abuser also employed emotional manipulation by withholding compliments and affection, creating an environment where she felt needy or weak for seeking validation and affirmation. This manipulation was designed to keep her emotionally dependent on the abuser's validation.

Additionally, her experience of walking on eggshells, fearing the abuser's outbursts and lectures, demonstrates the power dynamics at play. The abuser controlled the narrative by making her responsible for her own feelings while disregarding her emotional needs entirely.

Eleni:

"What did I do to make you stop loving me?" I asked. The response I received was chilling – a cold stare devoid of empathy as he observed me break down. ...This was my first real "aha" moment. Something was very wrong here. Something was very wrong with this person. "

At the start of our relationship, it felt like a fairytale. We went on trips, he showered me with affection, and I felt that I was living in a romance novel. Roughly a month knowing each other he asked me what type of wedding dress I would wear. Having experienced inconsistent communication from other men, ghosting etc. this consistency and flattery felt amazing and like I had finally found someone who was genuinely interested in forming a lifelong connection.

Also, this man was in therapy. How rare! However, the first time I saw a crack in his persona was during a car ride when he snapped at me. We were discussing our jobs, and I casually referred to him as an "influencer." His explosive reaction, correcting me as a "content creator," stunned me. He criticized influencers as talentless, and I was taken aback by the intensity of his response but I assumed that it was a sensitive topic. He quickly snapped back; it was so quick and unusual. Profusely apologizing for this behavior. Over time, I found myself ignoring these early red flags, convincing myself that his behavior wasn't as concerning as it seemed. However, things drastically changed when we bought a house and moved in together after knowing each other for less than a year. I later learned that he had wanted to buy a house for a while. It was probably never about me, he just wanted the image of a girl and a house. Any somewhat attractive and decently mannered girl would have probably done just fine.

The affectionate gestures soon gave way to subtle criticisms, corrections, and belittling remarks that I didn't recognize as abusive at the time. Initially, I thought he was joking, or maybe that he didn't understand that what he was saying was harmful. In one instance he mocked me and implied I was dumb for not being able to do math in my head. His focus then shifted towards his preferences for women which he would tell me about, highlighting characteristics that contradicted my own appearance — women who didn't wear much makeup or long fake nails, things that were not me at all. I began to change for him. When I would dress up and felt as though I looked nice to go out he said "it's okay I know you just do it for the patriarchy" he laughed off. I felt small and invalidated. I never dressed for anyone but me. Why say this instead of letting me know he found me beautiful?

This manipulation extended to our home life, where his preferences for cleanliness became increasingly stringent. I felt like no matter how hard I tried, I couldn't meet his standards, and the anxiety of falling short was overwhelming. He kept implying I wasn't clean. I had never heard this before. I was a clean person. As our relationship deteriorated, a cycle emerged, marked by emotional detachment, criticism, and sporadic affection. The moments of love-bombing grew rarer. A sense of unease had settled in, and I felt something was seriously wrong. He would sleep on the far end of the bed from me and we rarely even touched. Seeking more affection, I suggested we cuddle and hug more often, only to be met with the suggestion of scheduling these intimate moments (8am). He wanted to schedule time? Like an appointment? The clinical approach to something so personal was disconcerting and added to my confusion.

When I missed a session because I slept in he never initiated again. Seeing him walk out of the room. I remember asking him "is this torture?" He didn't respond.

I found out later that this is something similar he's done with other partners. In fact, I was warned by a mutual friend but ignored her warning because it wasn't happening to me at the time.

Slowly, cleaning at home became a battleground of control and criticism. Each unwashed dish or misplaced item gave him an opportunity to criticize me or tell me how I hadn't done something properly, even going so far as to show me photos of the pots I had supposedly failed to clean to his satisfaction. He zoomed in on them to show me where I had failed to clean them properly.

When I saw his car in the driveway, arriving earlier than anticipated, panic would set in as I scrambled to clean before his arrival. I knew the first thing he would mention was something being out of place.

In one particularly degrading event he told me to follow him to the bathroom so that I could flush the toilet in front of him. I said no, what type of request is that after all? He kept insisting that he show me what I had done and getting increasingly angry with me so I followed him. I walked with him to the bathroom and did what he asked. It made me feel like a child. I was so frustrated that I yelled and he seemed satisfied when I did. Appearing calm while I was dysregulated and feeling small. That evening I could feel his silent rage due to my reaction. He reverted his eyes from me that evening.

Small. This interaction made me feel smaller. That was the word that I kept repeating to myself and later to my therapist. He made me feel smaller. I felt like I was being reprimanded like a child. Little events like this. Little things constantly chipping away at me and my self esteem. As soon as I had gotten over one comment and he seemed to show affection again, then he would say or do something else to chip at me. And the cycle would repeat.

I began leaving conversations where I brought up an issue somehow apologizing. It was subtle ways he would talk down to me and posture in an authoritative way. Sometimes sitting across from me with a notebook writing down everything I said in interactions where I would express not liking something he had done. Telling me how I felt, that what I was feeling was stemming from something else and not really the core issue. I felt like he was my therapist.

I felt awful but didn't have the words or language yet to really vocalize why. One day finally something clicked and I left to stay at a hotel for a couple days and that's when I realized I felt better than I had in months. How I finally felt free. It was so odd. I had lived with a long term partner for almost six years before this and it was never this. I knew what living with a partner is supposed to feel like. And even though I had fought with partners before, they never made me feel small.

I came back and voiced my frustration. There were no attempts to mend the relationship by him. Just a cold and detached anger like ice. By the end of the relationship, I didn't recognize this person. He moved and behaved differently, it's so hard to explain. I later learned about how narcissistic people often "drop the mask" at the end of relationships so they sometimes don't appear like the person you knew. Maybe that's what was happening.

I found myself standing in the kitchen, tears streaming down my face, seeking answers from the person who had once professed their love for me. He was so cold.

"What did I do to make you stop loving me?" I asked. The response I received was chilling—a cold stare, devoid of empathy, as he observed me break down. He observed my pain as if it were a spectacle. Simply observing me cry while calmly pouring himself seltzer water.

At that moment, I felt small and vulnerable. It was as though he was watching paint dry. It was an inappropriate and detached response. His eyes were so dark and empty. I had never seen eyes like that before. This gaze was then accompanied by what looked like him being satisfied as he looked back from placing his seltzer water back into the refrigerator, leaving me shaken to my core.

I had never seen this response from another human being in my entire life.

No connection whatsoever. The best way I could describe it was that his stare was so cold and empty. I had never met anyone *empty* before. The little smirk, a slight uptick curling of the side of his mouth was terrifying.

This was my first real "aha" moment. Something was very wrong here. This wasn't just a toxic relationship. Something was very very wrong with this person.

He then went to the couch, sat down and berated me with a barrage of criticisms and blame. I stood frozen, drowning in tears, as he rattled off a list of my supposed faults and transgressions within the relationship as though he had prepared a list. The weight of his words and the contempt in his voice tore me down even further, leaving me clinging to the fragments of my self-esteem. He took this opportunity, during my vulnerability, to tear me down further. When I tried to speak up for myself he gave me a stern intimidating look implying I shouldn't dare to speak.

Seeing someone you love, treat you like that in a state of vulnerability and use it as a means to break you down more. Meet your vulnerability with such coldness and apparent satisfaction. I still have nightmares about that smirk. I felt like I was living in a horror movie, the ones where the couple moves into a home and the husband becomes possessed. It makes you start to think "who is this person?" Who is this total stranger, this evil person that I was sleeping next to for months?

I tried to mend the relationship many times. Sitting down, explaining how I felt and asking for some type of accountability. I was met with nothing like that at all. No apology, no acknowledgement. It was like trying to get water out of a stone. At this point I was just frustrated and confused. I was done. Or so I thought.

In a moment of weakness, which I currently understand was due to the trauma bond, I tried one last time to approach him. I flew back from SF to see him before he moved out. I reached out to touch his shoulder and he recoiled. Recoiled! As if I was disgusting. Not long ago he sent me love messages and now he recoiled? I was met with a look like he was disgusted with me and said "I would never want to be in a relationship with you". Disgusted? Then proceeded to blame shift and tell me everything was wrong with me. It was such a shift in who he was in the beginning. How was he able to "turn off" love so quickly?

I had never seen someone who lacked empathy before this experience or could be completely unaffected to someone's crying or turn off "love" so quickly.

Post separation was beyond difficult. I couldn't keep food down. I was grappling in my mind with the person who I thought he was and the one I met. It may not seem like much but when you've never experienced someone who's been empty and can watch you cry and seem to enjoy it before…especially someone you trusted had thought was good and who you gave your body to. Someone you thought cared about you and who you woke up to every day. It makes you feel violated.

It leaves you in shock and you have to rethink how you see the world. The monsters aren't under your bed. They're people closest to you. People you thought you could trust. People you've shared everything about yourself with because you thought they were safe. Ironically he plays horror games. I found myself thinking that he's the most terrifying horror. He's the real monster. The ones you don't see and that blend in too well. Who pretend to be nice caring guys. Those are the most terrifying. Those devoid of empathy who enjoy seeing someone broken down because it makes them feel more powerful. Like we deserve it. And people think they're easy to spot. They're not. Really they're not.

A month after, once he had moved out and I was still residing in the home, while I don't have a confession, I returned after a long trip to the locks having been changed. I was able to capture this being done and him on the ring camera footage. I requested the invoice from the locksmith and saw his signature. He refused having done this. Maybe he did, maybe he didn't. I've been too gaslit to know for sure anyway. I assume the worst though because he showed me he can be so evil. Even though he can come off sometimes as so aloof and almost childlike. It makes you think he doesn't know what he's doing. But I don't even know what else to call that reaction to someone's crying other than evil. So I call a spade a spade, and from now on assume the absolute worst intentions from that person.

— --

In the recounting of part of my story you can clearly see the idealization, devaluation and discard phases in a narcissistically abusive relationship. Initially, the relationship seemed like a fairy tale, with extravagant trips and affectionate gestures and moments of future faking. The rapid shift from romantic idealization to sudden criticism and correction signals the devaluation phase. The subtle insults and belittling remarks gradually erode a person's self-esteem and sense of worth, exemplifying the devaluation stage. And a discard (or in my case a bit of a reverse discard) where the narcissistic abuser's empathy seemingly switches off. Covert abusers don't outright call you stupid, however it's evident in these interactions that he was implying it. The clinical approach to intimacy, like scheduling hugs, and the demanding standards for cleanliness reflect the increasing control and manipulation that is typical in narcissistic relationships. Home becomes a battleground where a narcissistic person's dominance reigns supreme.

The exchange that follows is chilling—his detached gaze coldly observing me as I plead for answers. This stark contrast from the initial idealization and the subsequent transformation into an unfeeling entity left me bewildered and shattered. A clear sign of empathy deficits found in all narcissistic abusers. We all have similar stories when encountering narcissists. This is a hallmark narcissistic response to tears that many have reported.

This response is also emotional cruelty or the form of psychological abuse that Dr. Clare Murphy describes as "Emotional Unkindness".

Abusive individuals are skilled at using your vulnerabilities to their advantage. They take advantage of moments when you're feeling weak or vulnerable to actually abuse further and take that situation where you are vulnerable and kick you down because doing so gives them more power and control during that interaction. Which is at the core of abuse, what it all comes down to in an abusive dynamic. Power and control. This sort of psychological cruelty is a way to weaponize somebody's humanity against them, and maintain that semblance of power while making you smaller in the process.

Additionally, the narcissistic abuser combines emotional immaturity with an overpowering desire for control. Their preoccupation with controlling their environment and their belief that their way is the only way manifest in a toxic self-righteousness. The detrimental effects of their rigid outlook, leaves others feeling humiliated, oppressed, and dominated. By imposing their preferences onto others, they dismantle individuality.

Chapter 10

Therapeutic Charades

From evidence in the previous stories we discovered the chilling reality that it's actually quite common for narcissistic personalities to fly under the radar for many therapists, and can be psychologists by profession themselves. There are a number of red flags therapists should watch out for when dealing with a potential narcissistic person. Despite therapists' training and vigilance, many narcissistic people still manipulate even seasoned mental health professionals.

Firstly, clinicians should carefully consider when clients stay within a victim mentality a "woe is me the world is against me" thought process. This can be a red flag that the therapist is treating a vulnerable or covert narcissistic person. These people remain in victimhood in order to shift blame away from themselves and acquire supply in the form of sympathy. Typically a narcissistic person is never at fault. Always the victim, never an empowered survivor. I find in my own coaching and speaking with abuse survivors they are all strong capable people, and after our sessions have reclaimed their strength and slowly stand within it moving away from victimhood. They educate themselves about their experience, become stronger with better, more rigid boundaries, break out of people pleasing tendencies and sometimes go on to teach others through their own personal experiences with narcissistic people. It's an incredibly rewarding transformation to witness. However, from what I see narcissistic people perpetuate and exaggerate their victimhood as this garners narcissistic supply and sympathy.

Likewise, an apparent lack of empathy and exclusive focus on themselves is a red flag. Narcissistic individuals view others as mere extensions of themselves useful for validation. They show little authentic concern for how their behavior affects people. Everything is filtered through how it impacts the narcissistic person. Despite claiming to be victimized, clinicians may notice the narcissistic person moves on from apparent victimized situations surprisingly quickly, wherein the victim takes months if not years to recover from the abuse they experienced.

The victim often appears emotionally dysregulated, exhibits signs of PTSD and CPTSD, and often seems to be the "crazy" one while the abuser seems calm.

When assessing claims of abuse, understand that the victim may display what appear to be symptoms of emotional dysregulation or post-traumatic stress. Prolonged abuse often has psychological impacts that can leave victims seeming anxious, panicked and emotionally dysregulated. Abusers frequently use tactics to deliberately destabilize their partner's mental health over time as a means of control. They then point to this induced instability as evidence the victim is "crazy."

Meanwhile, the abuser's detached and calm facade provides a cover for further gaslighting the victim's perception of reality. See beyond these surface dynamics - a victim's emotional state and reactions may simply reflect the traumatic effects of abuse, while an abuser's composure masks a darker truth.

Narcissistic people also tend to shift blame excessively and have difficulty taking responsibility for their actions. There is always some external factor or person they point to as the real cause of any issues. This allows them to rationalize their hurtful behavior.

Other signals include exhibiting an attitude of entitlement, privilege, superiority or haughty behavior. Narcissistic people believe they are superior and should be recognized as such. Often in a therapist's sessions they may hear "my coworker is such an idiot, I talked to everyone and they agreed" (notice the triangulation here by stating everyone agrees along with a sense of superiority) or "they just won't listen to me, I'm obviously right" and similar such remarks.

Any attempt to directly or indirectly charm, intimidate, or otherwise manipulate the therapist should also trigger caution. If the client seems overly invested in controlling the therapist's opinion of them, it may point to a disordered narcissistic framework.

Additionally, covert narcissistic personalities are especially skilled at deception. Unlike overt narcissists, they don't present with obvious grandiosity or arrogance. Covert narcissistic people are much more subtle, often acting self-deprecating. This allows them to fly under the radar. Their manipulation is conveyed through passive aggression, victimhood narratives, and subtle sabotage such as "I'm so stupid" while also claiming to be superior in previous sessions. This duality is a red flag.

Additionally, narcissistic people are adept at targeting therapists' blind spots and biases. They quickly ascertain what given therapist is likely to respond to - whether sympathy, flattery, helplessness, or another tactic. They tailor their performance and stories accordingly. With an insightful therapist they may emphasize victimhood, while with a skeptical therapist they play up reform and progress.

Narcissistic people are also incredibly talented actors. Oscar worthy even. They so convincingly feign emotions and vulnerabilities that resonate with therapists' innate desire to help. Their capacity for lying is advanced enough to fool polygraph tests often because narcissistic people confabulate and believe their own narratives, fooling even a seasoned therapist into trusting their performance.

Even experts like Dr. Robert Hare, a psychologist and expert in psychopathy has been deceived occasionally. Therapists tend to underestimate a narcissistic person's capability for deceit. And after years in practice, overconfidence and complacency may set in. Skilled narcissistic personalities prey on these vulnerabilities in otherwise competent therapists.

Charm and flattery are typical tools in the narcissistic person's arsenal. They will often love-bomb their therapists by showering the therapist with praise, compliments, and admiration in order to gain favor with them. By making the therapist feel uniquely special and admired, the narcissistic person hopes to lower the therapist's guard and make them more susceptible to their agenda. Of course, this charm and adulation is not genuine - it is merely a means to an end. But to an unwary therapist, it can feel quite convincing.

Lying, omitting key details, and twisting the truth are other common manipulation techniques. The narcissistic person realizes that the therapist only hears their version of events and relationships. So the narcissistic person will selectively present information, omit, and even fabricate facts in order to control the narrative to their advantage. The narcissistic person will not mention accusations from their victims of them being abusive or lacking empathy. Which seasoned therapists would be able to decipher as key phrases indicating narcissistic traits.

Narcissistic people also excel at blame-shifting. By ascribing responsibility for all interpersonal problems and conflicts to third parties, the narcissistic person convinces the therapist of their innocence and garners sympathy. Of course, in reality the narcissistic person is often the one perpetrating emotional abuse. But the therapist hears only the narcissistic person's spin.

If their charm and falsehoods do not work, some narcissistic people will turn to discrediting the therapist. They may question the therapist's competence, qualifications, or basic grasp of psychology in order to undermine the therapist's authority. Some narcissistic people even resort to personal attacks if the therapis questions their false self-image - a last ditch effort to shut down the therapist's scrutiny.

Future faking is another common narcissistic ruse, where the narcissistic individual makes earnest promises to change without any actual intention to follow through. They pledge solemnly to be more caring, stop their narcissistic behaviors, or improve their relationships. But this is merely lip service, carefully crafted to tell the therapist what they want to hear. Once the therapist is convinced of their intent to change, they revert to their old ways.

Finally, triangulation is another favorite narcissistic ploy. The narcissistic person attempts to drive a wedge between the therapist and the narcissistic person's partner, family members, friends or others close to them. The narcissistic person feeds misinformation back to their inner circle in order to discredit the therapist, sow seeds of distrust, and maintain their scapegoat role. They may even try to charm and co-opt the therapist into aligning against the narcissistic person's perceived enemies and victimhood narrative.

Chapter 11

Recognizing Narcissistic Indifference

Have you ever experienced a moment when a narcissistic individual gives you a chillingly cold look as they watch you cry? It's that vacant expression that feels like the lights are on, but there's a dark void staring back. Maybe they fall sound asleep right next to you after they've hurt you as though nothing has happened? Perhaps they invalidate your feelings and say you're "too sensitive" or they may even become more aggressive. They may even accuse you of manipulating them by crying. These experiences can shake you to your core and reshape how you see the world. I'm sure before this experience, you weren't aware these reactions were possible or that there were people who could have deficits in human experiences like emotional empathy. You are not alone, this is a common experience many people who have been or are in relationships with potentially pathological narcissistic abusers describe. They may also experience this alongside a seemingly sadistic smirk also known as "duper's delight".

Within the intricate landscape of human psychology, a striking phenomenon known as instrumental and cognitive empathy emerges as a pivotal trait commonly exhibited by individuals with narcissistic individuals. This chapter delves into the depths of empathy, shedding light on how these personality types employ it and lack critical aspects of full empathy and the profound impact it has on interpersonal dynamics.

Indifference to emotional distress, lack of empathy, and an inability to connect emotionally can serve as clear and one of the hallmark indicators of narcissistic or even truly pathological people.

Empathy involves intricate neural mechanisms and cognitive processes that enable individuals to comprehend and share the emotions of others. Cognitive expert Frans de Waal delineates the diverse manifestations of empathy, from the altruistic to the apathetic. This exploration reveals the distinct categories within which empathy resides, encompassing those who genuinely care, those who withhold action, and those who manipulate.

According to a study by the Social Psychological and Personality Science, "results suggest that high levels of narcissism were associated with low levels of emotional contagion". Emotional Contagion describes the phenomenon of an automatic adoption of an emotional state of another person.

To be frank, when faced with someone's tears or emotional distress, those with very high narcissistic traits or with Narcissistic Personality Disorder (NPD) may exhibit a lack of emotional empathy and emotional contagion, leading to indifference. Experiencing this reaction can be jarring for the victim. Initially, the narcissistic individual may not recognize this as an inherent lack of emotional empathy, as they themselves may be unaware of the issue.

Emotional empathy refers to the ability to share another person's emotions, to feel with them and show compassion. However, narcissistic and psychopathic people typically struggle with this aspect of empathy due to their self-centeredness and limited capacity for emotional connection with others.

Narcissistic individuals often exhibit a pervasive pattern of self-centeredness and a lack of empathy. Their primary focus is on their own needs, desires, and ambitions, leaving little room for genuine emotional connection or concern for others. This emotional disconnect becomes particularly apparent when faced with the distress, sadness, or tears of those closest to them.

The atypical responses to your distress is indicative of a narcissistic person. Instead of receiving the expected supportive expression of concern, you might be met with this empty gaze. Whether you're in pain seeking sympathy, the narcissistic person offers no response. It's as if there's a disconnect between their ability to blend in and what they're feeling, which may be nothing.

In the fragile moments of vulnerability, the intricate web of a narcissistic individual's responses unfurls, revealing additional facets that perpetuate their harmful nature. Among these, outside of uncaring another two particularly distressing reactions stand out: anger and manipulation.

In the face of your emotional openness, the narcissistic person may resort to lashing out, their fiery outbursts serving as a defensive mechanism to shield their fragile ego from acknowledging your pain. In their self-absorbed universe, your emotional struggles are merely an inconvenience, a bothersome disruption to their grandiose narrative. As such, they belittle and undermine your valid emotional reactions, reducing your feelings to insignificance in an attempt to retain their illusion of control.

The Lack of Empathy:

Empathy consists of two main elements: Cognitive Empathy, which primarily involves thinking about other people's emotions, and emotional or affective empathy, which entails experiencing and sharing others' emotions. Together, these components encompass both the intellectual and emotional aspects of empathy. To elaborate, being empathic requires the ability to identify and comprehend the emotions of others (Cognitive Empathy) as well as the capacity to personally experience those emotions (Emotional Empathy). For instance, when observing someone in distress, you quickly acknowledge their sadness, while simultaneously experiencing a sense of sadness within yourself. In the case of narcissistic people, the capacity for genuine empathy is typically lacking. Their self-centered nature inhibits them from genuinely connecting with others' emotions, leading to an apparent indifference or disregard for the emotional states of those around them.

Cognitive empathy but deficits in emotional empathy affords them the ability to discern the emotions of others but not share or feel the emotions within themselves or share in the other's experience. Cognitive empathy diverges fundamentally from emotional empathy, as the former lacks the genuine intent to forge profound connections.

Individuals who wield cognitive empathy often emanate a charismatic charm, adept at convincing others of their authentic concern. Beneath this façade, however lies selfish desires. These individuals, accurately decipher behavioral cues, expressions, and tones to gauge others emotions, devoid of any emotional resonance.

In healthy relationships, emotional validation plays a crucial role in fostering connection and trust. It involves acknowledging and empathizing with the emotions of others, providing comfort, and creating a safe space for open expression. In contrast, narcissistic abusers will be disconnected, show indifference, invalidate or dismiss the emotions of others, downplaying their significance or even blaming the person experiencing distress. This emotional invalidation reinforces their self-centeredness and reinforces the emotional disconnect.

Encountering emotional indifference in a relationship can be deeply hurtful and damaging to one's emotional well-being. When someone fails to respond with empathy or concern during times of sadness or distress, it can lead to feelings of isolation, invalidation, and emotional neglect. Over time, this emotional neglect can erode the foundation of trust and intimacy, leaving the affected individual feeling isolated and unimportant in the relationship. Emotional disconnect, indifference to sadness, and a lack of empathy are warning signs that suggest highly narcissistic tendencies.

As we learned in a previous chapter, "Power & Control" , a lack of care, empathy, and cruelty is covert abuse on Dr. Clare Murphy's psychological abuse wheel categorized as "Emotional Unkindness".

Emotional connection and empathy are fundamental elements of healthy relationships, allowing individuals to support and understand one another on a deep level. M

This is also why some narcissistic individuals have shallow relationships or lose feelings for their intimate partners quickly. However there are a few other things that may cause this within a narcissistic individual. They include the grandiose false self, a need for admiration, and phenomena called splitting.

Shannon Petrovich, LCSW describes how narcissistic people use splitting. Splitting refers to a psychological defense mechanism that narcissistic people employ, in which they categorize people as either all good or all bad. This phenomenon leads to a dramatic shift in perception and treatment, resulting in the devaluation and cold lack of empathy towards those they once idealized. Experiencing this can be incredibly confusing, painful and devastating to the target of splitting.

In healthy relationships, it is normal to experience a range of emotions and perceptions towards others. People are seen as complex individuals with both positive and negative qualities. However, some individuals have difficulty tolerating the ambiguity and contradictions inherent in human nature, leading to a dichotomous "all-or-nothing" perspective.

The dramatic swing in mentality from idealizing to devaluing is a hallmark of splitting. During the idealization phase, the narcissistic person idolizes their partner, perceiving them as flawless, perfect, and meeting all their needs. This phase is often characterized by intense love, admiration, and a deep emotional connection. However, once the idealized image begins to crumble, the person is swiftly shifted into the "all bad" category.

This transition can occur without the usual qualifications that society generally considers necessary to devalue a person, such as infidelity or severe wrongdoing. In splitting, the devaluation is based on the internal emotional state of the individual, rather than on objective reality.

The ability to switch love off so abruptly and without egregious cause is indeed abnormal. In healthy relationships, love and attachment are based on a complex interplay of emotions, shared experiences, and understanding.

It takes time to erode or diminish genuine love and affection. This pattern of idealization and devaluation is deeply rooted in the individual's underlying psychological dysregulation. It serves as a defense mechanism to protect their fragile self and maintain a sense of control over their relationships. By splitting and devaluing others, they can avoid acknowledging their own imperfections, projecting blame onto their partners, and preserving a sense of superiority.

A lack of object constancy is closely linked to this phenomenon as well. Object constancy is the ability to maintain a consistent emotional connection and perception of someone, even when experiencing conflicting emotions or facing their imperfections. However, narcissistic individuals struggle with object constancy, which leads to splitting.

The lack of object constancy means that the person cannot integrate the positive and negative aspects of others into a cohesive whole. They have difficulties with what is referred to as "Whole Object Relations", instead they tend to view people as either all good (idealized) or all bad (devalued). This rigid splitting mechanism is driven by their fragile self-esteem and the need to protect their grandiose self-image.

When a narcissistic person, specifically those with NPD engage in splitting, they may idealize someone when they are meeting their needs or fulfilling their expectations. This idealization phase involves viewing the person as perfect, flawless, or the embodiment of their desires. However, if the person does something that triggers negative emotions or challenges the narcissistic abuser's self-image, the individual may suddenly shift to a devaluation phase. During this phase, the person is perceived as wholly negative, unworthy, and the source of all problems.

This extreme fluctuation between idealization and devaluation can be emotionally confusing and distressing for both the narcissistic abuser and those in their lives. It creates an unstable and unpredictable interpersonal dynamic, where relationships become highly volatile.

A key aspect of narcissistic behavior is the presence of discontinuous memory. They have difficulty retaining continuous memories, resulting in an inability to form true love and attachments.

Object constancy and whole object relations play significant roles in understanding narcissistic behavior. Whole object relations involve perceiving oneself and others in a stable and integrated manner, acknowledging both positive and negative qualities. They struggle with this stability, as they often have an all-or-nothing view, oscillating between idealization and devaluation. This is also known as black and white thinking.

One of the most striking aspects of splitting within the narcissistic abuser's lack of empathy towards their partner during the discard phase. Empathy, the ability to share another person's emotions, is a fundamental aspect of healthy human connection. However, for narcissistic abusers, emotional empathy is a foreign concept. Their emotional detachment and inability to empathize with the pain and suffering they inflict further magnify the psychological trauma experienced by the victim.

The repercussions of experiencing the effects of splitting in a relationship with a narcissistic abuser are profound. Victims often find themselves caught in a cycle of confusion, self-doubt, and emotional turmoil. The stark contrast between the idealization and discard phases can leave them questioning their own sanity and worthiness of love.

Chapter 12

Enablers & Flying Monkeys

Enablers are, in many ways, accomplices, though their complicity may not always be apparent. When someone outside a relationship becomes aware of one person abusing another and opts to do nothing but continue extending friendship to the abuser, they essentially endorse the abusive behavior. Enablers often rationalize their inaction by claiming it's not their business, but I want to stress that it is.

If someone in their circle harms another, and enablers don't address it, choosing to treat the abuser as they did before, they convey to the world that they don't uphold any standards for how people should treat each other. They demonstrate a willingness to associate with those who inflict harm on others, as long as they are not direct victims themselves.

This passivity sends a message to both the abuser and the community, indicating a lack of belief or seriousness regarding the abuse allegations and, even more disturbingly, an acceptance of the abuser's actions as long as they don't directly affect the enablers. Allowing an abusive person to remain part of the community without addressing their behavior essentially endorses it, providing the abuser with the social support and environment needed to perpetuate their abuse.

Many are unwilling to openly admit that they prioritize the safety of those close to them, willing to overlook harm to others to preserve their positive image of someone they care about. Enablers often employ flimsy excuses, such as "setting boundaries" or a reluctance to get involved, but true boundaries should never disregard victims while protecting perpetrators. This isn't boundary-setting; it's the misuse of therapeutic language to shield abusers.

Additionally, I will argue that confrontation by community members can often be the catalyst for abusers to examine and change their behavior. However paradoxically, research indicates that victims are often judged more harshly than the abusers by society, with enablers who stand by passively, doing nothing, equally contributing to the perpetuation of mistreatment. Although there may be rare situations where confronting an abuser poses safety concerns, more often, it is the discomfort of acknowledging that someone admired is capable of heinous behavior toward someone less significant to them that prevents enablers from taking action.

There are also enablers who become abusive themselves. "Flying Monkeys" is a term coined by Prof. Sam Vaknin to describe the individuals in the narcissistic abuser's life who blindly support the abuser and who then employ tactics like spying on the victim on their behalf and then relaying that information back to the abuser or harassing the victim. Also known as stalking.

Flying Monkeys should not be misconstrued as innocent bystanders. While many serve as enablers to the narcissistic individual, some go beyond passivity and actively engage in the victim's pain through stalking, manipulation, and other forms of abuse. These individuals don't merely bury their heads in the sand; they willingly step into the role of abusers by proxy.

For some Flying Monkeys, there's a perverse satisfaction in feeling needed, even if it means becoming instruments of the abusers manipulative agenda. They derive a sense of purpose from being drawn into other people's drama, often driven by their emotional attachment to the narcissistic person. Both Flying Monkeys and enablers can emerge from various circles, including family members, friends, or even the new romantic partner of the narcissistic person, all inadvertently contributing to the victim's suffering.

Chapter 13

Justice vs. Vengeance

So many people will preach love and light. Note, I am not one of those people. Victims wanting justice is normal. It does not make you a bad person or the one perpetuating abuse. However, justice is not a call for vengeance or punishment; it is a fundamental need for accountability and safety. It provides a sense of safety, a sense that our society values the protection of members others have harmed.

Victims after these relationships often feel unsafe, because when the person who violated them and disrupted their sanity remains unaccountable for their actions their sense of security erodes. They realize that there are countless others like that abuser, who are equally adept at evading detection by society. It is a paradigm shift of their entire worldview.

Additionally, the journey to recover from these relationships demand resources, time and often most victims are not able to access the support they truly need. When individuals endure abuse from those who claimed to love them and who they trusted whole-heartedly their entire worldview alters. It's not just the emotional scars they grapple with; it's also the deep betrayal trauma. So, when abusers can wreak havoc on someone else's life without justice it makes the world feel like a fundamentally unsafe place.

When we're told to 'just forgive' or 'why are you being so loud about this?,' it often feels like a subtle invitation to endure mistreatment silently, to avoid confronting someone about their behavior, and to maintain a status quo. It's as though victims are being asked to swallow their grievances and pretend they never occurred, as if they can simply be swept under the rug.

So let me reassure you. Being the bigger person doesn't mean turning a blind eye to abuse. True strength lies in acknowledging and addressing abusive behavior, in holding individuals accountable for their actions. If it's safe to do so, we must speak up against abusive behavior. And the burden for doing so shouldn't be only on the victim.

We must do it.

Chapter 14

Validation. No, You're Not Overreacting

"Narcissistic abuse" is a concept that encompasses a specific pattern of abusive behavior exhibited by individuals with highly narcissistic tendencies or other Cluster-B personality disorders. While it doesn't necessarily require the presence of a full-blown pathological narcissist, there exists a discernible and consistent framework of abuse, which we covered in the previous chapter "Narcissistically Organized Relationships".

Experiencing a narcissistically abusive relationship can be profoundly devastating, as they strip away your innocence and sense of security. This ordeal has the power to reshape your entire worldview and your perception of others. The resulting hyper vigilance leaves you perpetually wary of the world, as you realize that monsters do indeed exist. The jarring revelation that the very monsters that haunted our childhood fears are actual people—individuals we knew, trusted, and ever loved—inflicts a trauma that fundamentally alters who we are.

While some may struggle to empathize with victims of narcissistic abuse, dismissing them as exaggerating or seeking victimhood, the upheaval caused by having life's foundation and perception yanked from beneath you is indescribable. The core of your beliefs becomes uncertain. The harm inflicted by these individuals is immeasurable, and if quantifiable, I believe that the emotional and psychological torment they impose would unquestionably be classified as criminal. This is a form of domestic violence against the very essence of your being, shattering your mind and eroding your spirit.

Healing from narcissistic abuse is a complex process. The person who endured it must confront the harsh reality that the person they fell in love with was nothing more than an illusion. This creates cognitive dissonance within the victim's mind. Is the narcissistic person the kind loving person they fell in love with, or the cruel person who lacks empathy? Behind the narcissistic abuser's mask lies a manipulative individual who lacks empathy and seeks to control others. The victim becomes entangled with the false persona, unaware of the narcissistic abuser's true nature until later stages of the relationship, leading to emotional, psychological, and sometimes even physical harm.

This abuse often unfolds gradually, much like a frog placed in boiling water with the temperature rising imperceptibly. By the time you realize the change from idealization, devaluation and obvious forms of abuse it may be too late. The insidious nature of this abuse lies in its slow progression, rendering it difficult to detect. Hence, covert and narcissistic abuse not only inflicts harm through manipulation, but it also thrives on its ability to remain undetected until the individuals are deeply entwined.

Hindsight is twenty-twenty. And while early education about these narcissistic traits before deep involvement in a relationship can be immensely valuable, it is often the case that victims discover information about narcissism only once they have already experienced abuse. And you're not to blame- it's simply not common knowledge and the misconception that narcissistic abusers are easy to spot is incredibly inaccurate. You are not dumb, naive or flawed for "choosing" the abuser. You were groomed, manipulated and caught in a disordered relationship pattern caused by a deeply mentally unhealthy individual.

Chapter 15

Cognitive Dissonance in Narcissistic Relationships:

The concept of cognitive dissonance as it relates to narcissistic relationships is described by Dr. Sandra L. Brown, author of "Women Who Love Psychopaths" and President of the Association for NPD and Psychopathy Survivor Treatment Research and Education, provides valuable insights and experiences in understanding the phenomenon of cognitive dissonance in survivors of pathological love relationships.

Cognitive dissonance is a significant psychological phenomenon that emerges in survivors of narcissistic abuse. It arises when the mask of a narcissistic abuser begins to "slip" or come off all together, meaning they reveal their true nature which creates a stark contrast between their charming persona and abusive behaviors.

Survivors struggled to maintain a consistent view of their disordered partners, oscillating between conflicting thoughts, emotions, and perceptions about the relationship. This internal conflict arose from experiencing two distinct relationships with the same person—the charming, love-bombing persona and the abusive, disordered side. Thise who've experienced a these two terrifyingly stark differences in the perception of their partner find themselves torn between feelings of love and loathing, trust and distrust, and desire for the relationship and repulsion by its destructive nature.

Characterized by a disorder of social hiding, narcissistic/psychopathic traits involve individuals adept at concealing their true selves. These individuals wear masks of normality, often fooling even experts in the field. The term "Jekyll and Hyde" is used to describe the two distinct sides of the same person—the charming facade and the abusive reality. Survivors of narcissistic abuse may spend weeks, months, or even decades before they begin to unravel the other personas maintained by the pathological partner. The unmasking of the narcissistic abuser initiates a profound experience of cognitive dissonance for the survivor.

People with this Jekyll and Hyde persona often apear like to different people. Their victims may begin researching split personalities, bipolar or other such mental illnesses in order to grapple with the behavior they've experienced from the abuser. For example, the kind person you first met that would hold your hand as you both opened up about your difficult childhoods who was listening intently and empathetically, and the cruel abuser who seemed to exibit elation during your distress. Two very different people. One body.

Cognitive dissonance in narcissistic abuse involves holding contradictory belief systems simultaneously. Survivors find themselves grappling with conflicting emotions, such as love and loathing, trust and distrust, and acceptance and repulsion. The mind, naturally seeking harmony and balance, struggles to reconcile these opposing feelings, resulting in internal conflict. The discovery of the Jekyll and Hyde nature of the abusive partner triggers cognitive dissonance and marks the beginning of the survivor's traumatic journey. The trauma experienced in pathological relationships is distinct from other forms of trauma and contributes to the development of a unique form of cognitive dissonance.

Survivors of narcissistic abuse endure extensive gaslighting and manipulation before encountering cognitive dissonance. The unmasking of the narcissistic abuser further intensifies their mental turmoil, leaving them feeling mentally impaired and unable to discern reality. The cognitive dissonance experienced during this phase of the relationship takes a toll on the survivor's overall well-being, exacerbating symptoms of trauma and destabilizing their sense of self.

As the relationship progresses, and the mask continues to slip, the survivor's trauma deepens. The narcissistic partner may employ further gaslighting techniques to alter and manipulate the survivor's perception of reality. In some cases, the narcissistic abuser may swiftly abandon the relationship when exposed, leaving the survivor shocked and devastated.

Survivors of narcissistic abuse require comprehensive support and understanding to navigate the complexities of cognitive dissonance and its aftermath. The unique trauma inflicted by pathological relationships necessitates specialized therapeutic approaches. Mental health professionals and support networks must recognize the distinct nature of this trauma, differentiating it from conventional post-traumatic stress disorder (PTSD).

When the narcissist's facade crumbles, either by their choice or through exposure, their true, unpleasant traits come to the fore. As the need for pretense dissipates, the narcissistic abuser sees little reason to continue manipulating and deceiving their partner. Consequently, their nasty behaviors intensify, leaving the partner exposed to the full extent of their toxic personality.

So with the mask removed, the narcissistic abuser no longer feels compelled to maintain a facade of affection. The manipulation and façade of love tactics, previously used to keep the partner under their control, are abruptly discarded. Instead, the narcissistic abuser shifts gears, unleashing a torrent of toxic behaviors upon their partner. Emotional manipulation, gaslighting, verbal abuse, and devaluation may intensify during this stage. The partner finds themselves caught in the crosshairs of the narcissist's vindictiveness and cruelty.

The escalation of nasty behaviors often coincides with the narcissist's readiness to move on to a new target. Once the narcissistic abuser has depleted their current partner's emotional resources and extracted all possible benefits, they seek fresh sources of adoration, control, and validation. The partner becomes dispensable, no longer serving the narcissist's grandiose needs. Consequently, the narcissistic abuser disengages emotionally and psychologically, detaching from the relationship.

As the narcissistic abuser sets their sights on new conquests, they withdraw their efforts to maintain the partner's affection and compliance. This withdrawal of love can be disorienting and emotionally devastating for the partner, who now grapples with feelings of abandonment and confusion. Questions arise if the whole relationship was fake and "Who is this cruel person?" is common as the narcissistic person's indifference and lack of investment in the relationship become apparent, leaving the partner questioning the authenticity of their past experiences.

Chapter 16

Trauma Bonds

So, what are Trauma Bonds? In short, a trauma bond is an emotional attachment a victim forms to the abuser. This bond makes it extremely difficult for the victim to leave their abuser. As a coach who works with victims of domestic violence, I frequently encounter trauma bonding.

Trauma bonds develop through intermittent reinforcement. The abuser alternates between being affectionate and being cruel or violent. This conditioning strengthens the victim's emotional reliance on the abuser. The victim becomes addicted to the "highs" of the good times, which increases their tolerance for the "lows" of the bad times.

The biochemical process of trauma bonding mirrors that of a gambling addiction. In both cases, the brain experiences alternating periods of high stress and reward which create an addictive attachment. With trauma bonds, cortisol initially spikes during incidents of abuse, triggering a fight-or-flight response. When the abuser then shows affection, the brain releases dopamine and opioids, causing pleasure and relief.

This rollercoaster of cortisol and dopamine forms an addiction to the unpredictability of the reward. The victim becomes hooked on chasing the small "wins" of affection to balance the mistreatment. Just as a compulsive gambler seeks the dopamine rush of occasional jackpot wins despite habitual losses, the trauma bond victim pursues dopamine during the honeymoon period at the expense of prolonging the abuse cycle.

Trauma bonds often involve three key components:

1. A power imbalance where one person has more control
2. Intermittent positive and negative treatment leading to emotional addiction
3. Isolation from other support systems so the victim depends solely on the abuser

Victims in trauma bonded relationships crave emotional intimacy during the "good" times when the abuser showers them with affection. But when the abuse recurs, they suffer withdrawal symptoms like anxiety, depression, and confusion. This creates a constant yearning and fixation on the abuser.

Abusers deliberately induce trauma bonding through tactics like love bombing, gaslighting, and Stockholm syndrome grooming. Love bombing involves an initial display of excessive attention and affection to influence the victim. Gaslighting refers to the abuser manipulating the victim into doubting their own feelings, perceptions, and sanity. Stockholm syndrome grooming is when the abuser combines positive reinforcement and abuse to gain total control. These methods further entrap the victim in the unhealthy dynamic.

Trauma bonds develop through several stages:

Stage 1: Idealization

In the beginning, the connection feels deep, intense, and genuine. The abuser showers the victim with flattery, gifts, and nonstop attention. The victim feels appreciated, seen, and understood.

Stage 2: Bonding

The abuser systematically gains the victim's trust through reliability and emotional intimacy. The victim starts feeling dependent on the abuser for validation.

Stage 3: Devaluation

The abuse begins slowly through criticism and blame. The abuser becomes demanding and insists on changes in the victim's normal behavior or relationships.

Stage 4: Disorientation

The abuser utilizes gaslighting and emotional manipulation to confuse and disorient the victim. The victim doubts their own feelings and perceptions.

Stage 5: Resignation

The victim concludes that fighting the abuser is futile. They resign themselves to compliance in hopes of avoiding conflict.

Stage 6: Hostage

The victim loses their sense of self and walks on eggshells to avoid the abuser's criticism and anger. Any attempts at independence result in retaliation.

Stage 7: Addiction

The victim feels unable to leave despite the unhappiness and damage to their self-esteem. The biochemical pull of the trauma bond prevails.

This understanding of trauma bonding is a fairly recent discovery in how trauma bonds function, and how they are much like an addiction, creating biochemical and psychological dependence we can better help victims heal. Whereas before people assumed victims were not intelligent or would ridicule victims who would continuously go back to the abuser after mistreatment, we now have a firm grasp of the mental workings behind this behavior. The abuse victim experiences withdrawal symptoms when separated from their abuser. The brain releases opioids and dopamine during the honeymoon phases which become craved.

The alternating cruelty and kindness of the abuser creates an addictive attachment for the victim. The abuse corrodes the victim's self-worth over time. The victim blames themselves and makes excuses for their abuser's behavior.

The isolation imposed by the abuser also bolsters the trauma bond. With no outside perspectives offering validation, the victim questions their own judgment. Shame and self-blame keep the victim trapped in the cycle.

To fully break free of a trauma bond, it is essential to go through a period of detoxification from the abuser. This involves completely removing oneself from the abusive relationship, cutting off all contact, and avoiding places the abuser may show up.

This is because abusers often use persuasive language to lure victims back in during the separation process. It causes more confusion and delays healing by keeping you trapped in their mental fog. Seeing or communicating with the abuser, even briefly, can quickly re-engage the trauma bond. Victims may experience emotional cravings and withdrawal symptoms if exposed to the abuser.

Staying away from the abuser requires determination and commitment. It may mean changing jobs, getting a new phone number, and severing mutual social connections. This detox period allows the brain to reset and break free of the emotional addiction.

With time and zero contact, trauma bonds weaken and lose their grip. The victim can regain clarity and reconnect to their core self, values, and desires. Detoxing from the abuser is essential to fully reclaiming one's life after escaping trauma bonding.

Chapter 17

Intimacy In Narcissistic Relationships

In the realm of romantic entanglements involving narcissistic people, the landscape of sex and intimacy takes on an utterly abnormal and perplexing form.

In this chapter, we delve into the intricate world of narcissistic relationships, specifically focusing on the perplexing dynamics surrounding intimacy and sex that is often seen in these relationships. I aim to shed light on the struggles faced by both partners within a narcissistic relationship and provide a roadmap for understanding.

In the narcissistic abuser's mind, intimacy and sex are two separate entities that can often conflict with one another. Intimacy, with its emotional depth and connection, dampens their sexual desires, creating a paradoxical struggle within the relationship. As such, narcissistic people may objectify their partners or refrain from intercorse all together.

The Madonna-Whore complex is a common occurrence narcissistic personalities face. This psychological phenomenon casts a long shadow over the intimate connections with narcissistic abusers, affecting the dynamics of sex and emotional intimacy in profound ways. I want to highlight the intricacies of this complex interplay, exploring how the narcissistic abuser's perception of their partner evolves, leading to a troubling shift in attraction, and ultimately, how this affects the victim.

The Madonna-Whore complex, initially conceptualized by Sigmund Freud, is a psychological dilemma that manifests in an individual's inability to maintain sexual arousal within a committed relationship. The person with this complex reconciles the two facets of women in their lives – the Madonna, representing purity, nurturing, and motherhood, and the Whore, representing sensuality, desire, and sexual allure. For narcissistic abusers, this complex often takes center stage in the sexual aspects of the relationship.

In the early stages of the relationship, narcissistic abusers are known for their love-bombing tactics. They shower their victims with attention, affection, and seemingly genuine admiration. During this phase, the victim is elevated to a pedestal, often seen as the embodiment of their ideal partner – a perfect blend of the Madonna and the Whore. In the eyes of the narcissistic abuser, the victim is alluring, captivating, and sexually desirable. Their sexual connection is intense, seemingly unparalleled, and a critical tool for binding the victim emotionally.

As the relationship progresses, the narcissistic abuser gradually transitions into the devaluation phase. This is where the trouble begins. The abuser's perception of their partner starts to shift, and the idealized image constructed during the love-bombing phase begins to crumble. They no longer view their partner as a multi-dimensional individual but rather as a vessel to fulfill their emotional and physical needs.

The Madonna-Whore complex plays a pivotal role in this shift. The abuser's perception of their partner starts to lean more heavily towards the Madonna archetype. As they devalue their victim, they begin to see them as motherly– a stark departure from the passionate, sexually alluring figure they were initially attracted to. This shift in perception triggers a troubling transformation in their sexual desire.

The loss of sexual attraction experienced by narcissistic abusers can be distressing and confusing for the victim. It is not uncommon for the abuser to withdraw from sexual intimacy or display a significant decline in sexual interest. This shift is rooted in their perception of the victim as a maternal figure rather than a sexual one.

The narcissistic abuser may perceive sex with their partner as "wrong" due to the increasing association with the Madonna archetype. This internal conflict intensifies their cognitive dissonance, as they struggle to reconcile their desire for sexual gratification with their evolving perception of their partner.

In this stage, the narcissistic abuser may deploy emotional manipulation and gaslighting tactics to further exacerbate the victim's confusion and insecurity. They may accuse the victim of being overly sexual or promiscuous, shaming them for desires they once encouraged. Simultaneously, they may withhold affection, intimacy, or validation, deepening the victim's emotional turmoil. The victim begins to grapple with feelings of inadequacy, rejection, and confusion. They may yearn for the passionate connection they once shared with the abuser, struggling to understand the abrupt shift in the abuser's perception of them.

Additionally, in some cases the intricate realm of narcissistically organized relationships, where power dynamics and manipulation reign supreme, sex takes on a unique and often bewildering form.

For the narcissistic partner, sex serves a dual purpose acquiring and capturing their partner while simultaneously feeding their own ego.

However, lurking deep beneath the surface of the narcissistic abuser's sexual prowess lies a paradoxical resentment towards intimacy and vulnerability. Inevitably, the narcissistic abuser may reach a point where they deem the relationship secure enough to discard the facade of sexual intimacy. Sex becomes a chore, a mere maintenance activity that clashes with their values and ideology. The partner is left bewildered and frustrated, longing for the resumption of a passion that has now been extinguished.

Likewise, Indigo Stray Conger, a certified sex therapist and writer for Choosing Therapy, points out that this phenomenon may also be attributed to the emotional disconnect often experienced by narcissistic people

"In terms of adult attachment styles, men with Narcissistic Personality Disorder (NPD) tend to be on the far end of the attachment spectrum, under Avoidant Attachment. Avoidant attachers have difficulty connecting emotionally during sex, often using masturbation in lieu of sex with partners and having less interest in sexual connection with partners as relationships become long term. Men with NPD, in addition to these factors, tend to use sex as a way to achieve self-esteem and emotional manipulation," explains Conger."

For some narcissistic abusers, sex is often seen as a transaction rather than an expression of love or genuine intimacy. They may view their partners as objects whose primary purpose is to fulfill their sexual desires. In this transactional mindset, the abuser believes that by providing certain benefits or meeting their partner's material or emotional needs (albeit superficially), they are entitled to sex as a form of repayment. This approach reduces the depth and authenticity of the sexual connection, turning it into a mere bargaining tool within the relationship.

They may use sex as a means of exerting control, emotional manipulation, or even punishment. If their partner withholds sex or expresses discomfort, the abuser may react with anger, guilt-tripping, or passive-aggressive behavior, thereby coercing them into complying with their desires. In such scenarios, the victim's consent is often invalidated, and the abuser's sense of entitlement becomes more pronounced.

One important thing to remember when dealing with a narcissistic individual sex is never healthy or normal, and does not equate to true intimacy. Narcissistic abusers can play elaborate games of push and pull, creating tension and instability to keep you hooked. This constant rollercoaster of emotions takes a toll on your mind and body, resulting in anxiety and constant ups and downs.

Chapter 18

Recognizing Narcissism in Legal Proceedings

Legal proceedings set a unique list of challenges when dealing with individuals demonstrating narcissistic traits. From their attempts to uphold a meticulously crafted public self-image to calculated strategies designed to elongate the legal process, attorneys must be attuned to the telltale signs that set these cases apart.

Narcissistic individuals exhibit behavior patterns that can alert attorneys to their presence. Frank Vendt, Esq provides a list of qualities narcissistic people employ that could be potential red flags that your client or the opposing client is highly narcissistic. Some of these include "making last-minute changes to proposed settlement agreements", "harassing their victim", "deliberately delaying decisions or meetings"and "Stalking you: Narcissists may stalk you in order to keep tabs on you or intimidate you". The stalking may be done in person or more commonly online. All of these tactics are meant to enact control and superiority. Additional red flags include attempts to silence the victim to preserve their self-image, deliberate attempts to prolong the legal process, feigned cooperation followed by withdrawal, and inserting un-agreed upon stipulations among others. Narcissistic individuals embark on a campaign to elongate the divorce proceedings for a multitude of reasons, all rooted in their insatiable need for control.

These individuals often seek to silence victims in order to uphold their self-image through coercing victims into signing various forms of "hush" agreements like, non-disparagements, confidentiality clauses and other "gag order" language. Narcissistic individuals are incredibly image focused. This behavior stems from their deep-seated insecurity, causing them to avoid any threats to their reputation and uphold their well crafted public persona.

Furthermore, narcissistic individuals frequently employ strategies to extend legal proceedings. This might involve unnecessary disruptions, frivolous motions, and continuous negotiations. Such tactics aim to maintain control and attention. An erratic pattern of cooperation and sudden withdrawal is common among narcissistic individuals. This approach serves to destabilize opponents, fostering confusion and emotional turmoil while retaining an element of control. Manipulating the process, narcissistic individuals may introduce unexpected stipulations or modifications. This tactic asserts dominance and aims to compel opponents to acquiesce.

Navigating the intricate landscape of court and legal proceedings with narcissistic individuals can prove profoundly exhausting. It's crucial to maintain a stance of non-reactivity while remaining resolutely goal-oriented. Anticipating an extended and challenging battle, it's imperative to bolster your inner strength mentally, physically, and financially, in order to effectively counter the tactics employed by these individuals. Documenting a comprehensive record of their manipulative behaviors, abusive actions, financial improprieties, and any other transgressions is a strategic move that can potentially prove invaluable during court proceedings. Moreover, preserving a sense of composed equanimity serves as a powerful deterrent against the narcissistic person's deliberate attempts to incite reactions and seize control over your emotional state.

Chapter 19

A Tale As Old As Time: The Dark Fairytale Between The Narcissist & Empath

The myth of Narcissus and Echo, an ancient Greek tale, holds a powerful metaphor that can be applied to the relationship dynamics between a narcissist and an empath. In this myth, Echo represents the empath, while Narcissus embodies the narcissist. By examining the story's elements, we can gain insights into the intricate and often destructive dynamics that can unfold between these two personality types.

So, I apologize, you see...I'm Greek. And to quote Gus Portokalos a la "My Big Fat Greek Wedding" "Give me a word, any word, and I show you that the root of that word is Greek."

The word "narcissist" finds its roots in Greek mythology, specifically in the myth of Narcissus. Sigmund Freud, used the term "narcissism" originally referred to a natural stage in childhood development but came to represent a disorder when it persists into adulthood.

According to Dr. Anabel Gonzalez's article titled "Narcissism as a Consequence of Trauma and Early Experiences," she asserts that individuals with narcissistic tendencies are unable to outgrow this developmental stage naturally. This stagnation occurs as a result of trauma hindering their normal emotional growth and development.

By examining the myth, we can delve deeper into the essence of narcissism and its lasting impact.

The Story of Echo and Narcissus:

One day, Echo encountered Narcissus, the exceptionally beautiful son of a river god and water nymph. Narcissus, having been foretold that he would live a long life only if he never truly knew himself, grew into a proud youth who attracted numerous admirers but left a trail of broken hearts in his wake. Echo, consumed by longing, followed Narcissus silently, unable to initiate a conversation as she was cursed by Hera to only be able to echo the words of others.

When Narcissus heard Echo's approach, he questioned her identity, to which she could only respond with a repeated "you," desperately attempting to hold him. Irritated, Narcissus rejected Echo and declared his preference for solitude. Devastated, Echo pleaded for his love but was met with harsh rejections. Echo's heart grew heavy, her body frail, until all that remained was her voice, echoing through vast and desolate places.

Narcissus, having cruelly rejected Echo, also faced the consequences of his actions. Ameinias, another individual who had been spurned by Narcissus, had prayed to the goddess of revenge, Nemesis, seeking justice. Witnessing Echo's tragic fate, Nemesis orchestrated Narcissus's downfall. Nemesis guided Narcissus to a reflective pool where he encountered his own reflection, an exquisitely beautiful image he had never before seen with such clarity. Enchanted by his own likeness, Narcissus became fixated, spending his days exploring every angle and admiring his reflection in the moonlight. However, he soon realized that his love was unrequited, as his reflection disappeared whenever he attempted to embrace it. Many would assume this means he was vain and in love with himself. However, narcissus believed that he was staring and in love with another person. That person reflected back to him. This is a wonderful representation of the narcissist's strive for ideal love and perfection that may not exist.

Consumed by unfulfilled longing, Narcissus wasted away, refusing sustenance and withering physically. Eventually, all that remained of him was a white and yellow flower, forever bent towards its own reflection. From that moment on, the flower became known as the narcissus. The myth of Narcissus and Echo offers a poignant allegory for understanding the complex dynamics between narcissists and empaths. While the narcissist is preoccupied with idealized love, the victim, like echo, wishes the narcissist would truly see them instead of the reflection of the ideal.

The myth highlights the consequences of unchecked narcissism, emphasizing the destructive impact on both the narcissistic abuser and those caught in their orbit. Like Narcissus, narcissists do not experience true love but rather Idealization and Devaluation and are in search for this ideal love which is a fantasy, a watery illusion.

Chapter 20

Are They Really A Narcissist?

Covert Narcissists, Sociopaths and Psychopaths often do not portray themselves as self-centered and unempathetic right away. When you first meet them, they may seem kind, humble, and in many cases almost childlike, which was the case for me. But as the relationship progresses, you will notice subtle changes, subtle bids for power, dominance and control. They will morph into someone self-centered and uncaring, which is their true selves. They pretend to be vulnerable to get others to extract narcissistic supply or solidify their mask of a good kind and even meek person. In reality, these people lack empathy, are condescending, and self-centered.

Throughout this book I've made a point to use terms narcissistic people, individuals and narcissistic abusers as frequently as possible. However, let's now talk about identifying NPD specifically. In the DSM-5 (Diagnostic and Statistical Manual of Mental Disorders, 5th edition), narcissistic personality Disorder (NPD) is characterized as a condition where individuals display many traits including self-centeredness and a lack of empathy.

I want to stress that I'm not a clinician, so in this chapter I want to cover pathological narcissism by sharing knowledge from experts in the field of narcissism and other disorders. Dr. Mark Ettensohn, an expert in the field of narcissism, advocates for the DSM-5 Alternative Model for NPD, which offers a more comprehensive understanding of this disorder and which may be better at recognizing covert and vulnerable representations. He writes more about his understanding of individuals with this condition through his book, 'Unmasking Narcissism: A Guide to Understanding the Narcissist in Your Life' and I personally found his insights to be both enlightening and refreshing.

He states that the DSM-5 attempts to rectify some of the shortcomings of the previous edition by proposing an alternative model for NPD as the nine criteria are primarily seen in grandiose representations of the disorder, but fails to address characteristics of vulnerable or covert representations.

If you're reading about covert abuse, there is a possibility that you have been interacting with a covert narcissist so let's explore this alternative diagnostic model. This model recognizes impairments in interpersonal functioning and the presence of pathological personality traits as essential features of the disorder.

This model defines NPD as manifested by characteristic difficulties in two or more of the following areas:

NPD – An Alternative Model:

Identity: Excessive reference to others for self-definition and self-esteem regulation; exaggerated self-appraisal—inflated or deflated or vacillating between extremes; emotional regulation mirrors fluctuations in self-esteem.

Self-direction: Goal-setting based on gaining approval from others; personal standards are unreasonably high in order to see oneself as exceptional, or too low based on a sense of entitlement; often unaware of own motivations.

Empathy: Impaired ability to recognize or identify with the feelings and needs of others; excessively attuned to reactions of others, but only if perceived as relevant to self; over- or underestimates own effects on others.

Intimacy: Relationships largely superficial and exist to serve self-esteem regulation; mutuality constrained by little genuine interest in others' experiences and predominance of a need for personal gain.

Grandiosity: Feelings of entitlement, either overt or covert; self-centeredness; firmly holding to the belief that one is better than others; condescending towards others.

Attention seeking: Excessive attempts to attract and be the focus of the attention of others; admiration seeking.

To begin with, it's worth noting that while Narcissistic Personality Disorder is more commonly diagnosed in men, Borderline Personality Disorder and Histrionic Personality Disorder are disorders that are typically diagnosed more frequently in women. Individuals with each of these disorders may have a higher likelihood of engaging in abusive or socially erratic behavior.

In a thought-provoking video by Dr. Craig Malkin "Narcissistic, Psychopathic, and Borderline Personalities : Key Differences", a clinical psychologist and lecturer for Harvard Medical School, he delves into the variances between narcissism, psychopathy, and borderline personality disorder. With his expertise in the field and his book "Rethinking Narcissism," Dr. Malkin aims to help individuals comprehend and navigate these complex traits within their relationships.

Cluster-B disorders have distinct motivational differences. Dr. Malkin provides insights into how these disorders may manifest in relationships. Extremely narcissistic abusers may initially appear confident, but their insecurities and need for self-enhancement may lead to entitlement or aloofness/withdrawal as the relationship progresses. In contrast, individuals with psychopathy focus on establishing control and power dynamics early on. They may attempt to manipulate situations or ignore their partner's preferences to maintain a position of dominance. Borderline personality disorder manifests through fear and reactivity, with individuals oscillating between a desire for connection and the fear of being harmed or controlled.

Dr. Malkin emphasizes that while there can be overlaps between these disorders, it is crucial to recognize their unique central concerns.

ASPD is also often mistaken for Narcissistic Personality Disorder. ASPD referring to those that could be classified as psychopaths and sociopaths are more common than people realize and no, they're not all out here committing murders. Psychopathy has been categorized into two factors. Factor 1 is often believed to have a biological origin, while Factor 2 psychopathic traits are thought to potentially arise after exposure to childhood trauma.

The research into ASPD and statistics tied to those with high psychopathic traits has primarily been conducted in the prison population, meaning that the behavior recorded exemplifies the extreme manifestations of these conditions. It's this generalization that all those with ASPD must be axe murderers which narrows our perception of who these people are and how they behave in society.

In fact, research shows that one in five business leaders have very high psychopathic traits and could be considered full psychopaths.

Additionally, did you know that individuals can experience more than one disorder simultaneously? This phenomenon is referred to as comorbidity, where two or more disorders coexist within an individual. Comorbidity may arise due to shared underlying factors or confounding variables that contribute to the manifestation of multiple disorders. It's essential to understand that comorbidity does not imply a causative relationship between the disorders; rather, it highlights their co-occurrence. Those with psychopathy or more psychopathic traits may be more cold, detached and calculative while those with more narcissistic traits may appear more emotionally volatile.

Could it be related to ADHD? This question arises many times from my clients. Because some individuals with ADHD may exhibit certain outwardly narcissistic behaviors, such as love bombing, where they might hyper fixate on a specific person but I want to stress they are not the same. Narcissists and those with ASPD lack affective empathy.

Interestingly, research indicates that ADHD and NPD can co-occur, and this combination surprisingly occurs quite frequently.

However, it's essential to clarify that the takeaway here is not to label everyone with ADHD as a narcissist. Instead, the point is that both conditions can and often do commonly occur together.

*Often people who are narcissists wonder if they also have ADHD. Sometimes even ADHD is used to explain the narcissistic behavior. Well here's a startling fact ADHD and narcissism overlap **60%** of the time" –Kerry McAvoy, PhD*

ADHD and personality disorders frequently co-occur alongside other Axis I disorders. This striking overlap between ADHD and personality disorders becomes particularly evident within incarcerated populations. A staggering 96% of incarcerated adults with ADHD had a lifetime history of antisocial personality disorder (Psychopathy, Sociopathy). Furthermore, other types of personality disorders were disproportionately prevalent within this group, including borderline (74%), paranoid (74%), narcissistic (65%), obsessive-compulsive (52%) and avoidant (48%).

Unfortunately, there's a notable dearth of clinical trials evaluating management strategies for personality disorders in general, and even less so when considering comorbid cases with ADHD.

ADHD is characterized by executive functioning deficits, such as difficulties with attention, organization, and planning. These deficits may contribute to challenges in maintaining healthy relationships and regulating self-esteem, potentially increasing the likelihood of narcissistic behaviors.

However, adverse childhood experiences such as trauma or neglect, may increase the risk of developing both narcissistic traits and ADHD symptoms. Shared environmental factors or early life experiences may contribute to the co-occurrence of these disorders.

Understanding the potential overlap between narcissism and ADHD can have important implications for clinical practice. The intersection of narcissism and comorbidity with other disorders, presents a thought-provoking area of exploration.

Chapter 21

Does it Matter?

As survivors delve deeper into the intricate world of narcissism and its comorbidity with other disorders, it becomes essential to shift our focus from the diagnostic labels to the core issue at hand: the abuse. While understanding the nuances and characteristics of narcissistic Personality Disorder (NPD) can be enlightening, it is important to remember that the impact of an abusive relationship extends far beyond a diagnostic checklist.

The label of "narcissist" has gained significant attention in recent years, and it has become somewhat of a buzzword in popular culture. While recognizing unhealthy patterns and toxic behaviors is crucial for personal growth and healing, it is equally important to emphasize that the label itself is not the focal point. What truly matters is the abuse endured within the relationship.

Abuse knows no specific diagnostic category. It transcends labels and manifests in various forms—emotional, verbal, psychological, physical, and sometimes even financial. The effects of abuse on a person's mental and emotional well-being can be devastating, regardless of whether the abuser meets the diagnostic criteria for NPD or any other disorder. Understanding the abuse dynamics and their profound impact is the key to healing and breaking free from the cycle.

In many cases, individuals who have been subjected to abuse find themselves caught up in a whirlwind of confusion and self-doubt. They may question their own judgment, blame themselves for the relationship's failures, or struggle to comprehend the manipulative tactics employed by their partners. The label of narcissism can provide a framework for understanding some of these dynamics, but it is essential to remember that abuse is not limited to a single personality disorder.

What matters most is recognizing the harmful patterns within the relationship and acknowledging the emotional, psychological, and physical toll they have taken. It is about validating one's own experiences and understanding that abuse is never acceptable or deserved, regardless of the label attached to the abuser.

So, it is not about the label; it is about acknowledging the abuse and working towards healing. By focusing on the core issue — the abuse itself — we can break free from the cycle, foster understanding, and arm ourselves with understanding so as to spot these behaviors moving forward.

Chapter 22

Healing From Narcissistic Relationships

Healing from narcissistic relationships is a deeply personal and transformative journey. It requires self-reflection, self-compassion, and a commitment to your own well-being. In this chapter, I will take you through the essential steps I personally undertook to transform into a survivor to begin the healing process from this relationship bolstered by research and my work with clients who have undergone the same journey. Until now, you have been subjected to victimization and abuse. You now have the opportunity to break free from this role. Being a victim is a distressing experience that leaves us feeling powerless and at the mercy of others. If it persists, this sense of helplessness can become ingrained in our identity. However, our lives extend far beyond the things that happen to us, and often, these experiences can even fuel our inner strength.

After these experiences you may be tempted to empathize or rationalize away the abuser's behavior. It is natural to want to believe that others have pure and loving intentions, assuming that they share our own motives. This is a form of positive psychological projection. However, this assumption is flawed. It is important not to project your goodness on to others or assume that other people's intentions align with yours, as this leaves you vulnerable and unsuspecting, making you an easy target for victimization.

As you awaken to the reality of abusive patterns and move away from denial, it is important to focus on a person's actions rather than their words. This will provide valuable insight into their true motivations and intentions. Additionally, alongside understanding abusers and their tactics, it is vital to have self-awareness. Being honest with yourself about your personality and vulnerabilities allows you to better protect yourself as you move forward. For instance, if you tend to overcompensate for others' shortcomings or engage in people-pleasing, consciously stopping this behavior even if it feels uncomfortable, is necessary. This will help you refrain from carrying the weight of others and protect yourself by avoiding individuals who exploit your vulnerabilities. As a recovering people-pleaser, I absolutely understand how this is more easily said than done.

While there is no one-size-fits-all approach to healing, the following steps can provide a roadmap for your recovery.

First, let's outline what you may experience right after leaving this relationship. Healing from narcissistic abuse is a multifaceted journey, encompassing fourteen distinct stages. The first seven are the stages of grief while the next seven help you heal and reclaim your life after acceptance.

While many are familiar with the five stages of grief, recovering from narcissistic abuse uniquely has seven stages as people are left grieving a person who is still alive but realized never truly existed.

Stage 1: Devastation

Your journey begins with devastation. It's that pivotal moment when you witness the narcissistic abuser's mask slipping and experience the painful discard, typically characterized by cruelty and hurtful behavior. This stage is a stark awakening to the reality of the abusive relationship, leaving you emotionally shattered.

Stage 2: Denial

Denial creeps in as you grapple with the shock of what you've endured. Self-doubt and self-gaslighting become routine, leading you to question the validity of your experiences. Euphoric recall, where you reminisce about positive moments with the narcissistic abuser, further compounds this phase, making you question whether the abuse was as severe as it seemed.

Stage 3: Education

Education is a vital turning point. You embark on a quest for knowledge, seeking to understand the intricacies of narcissistic abuse. You may find yourself scouring the internet for information on the symptoms, behaviors, and stages of narcissistic relationships. This phase helps you make sense of your experience and recognize the patterns of abuse.

Stage 4: Anger

Anger is a natural response to having your boundaries violated and enduring severe mistreatment. This stage is a healthy release of pent-up emotions. When working with clients, I encourage survivors to progress beyond anger to a point of disgust, where you recognize the narcissistic abuser's behavior as utterly reprehensible. You will be disgusted by the way they treated you and will never want to encounter them again.

Stage 5: Depression/Grief

Even though the narcissistic abuser treated you poorly, you may experience a profound sense of loss and sadness. The trauma bond still lingers, leading to conflicting emotions. Depression is normal during this phase, as you grapple with the aftermath of the abusive relationship, a loss of the life you may have had, the promises the narcissistic abuser never kept, and the grief and loss of a person who never existed.

Stage 6: Bargaining

Similar to the classic stages of grief, bargaining emerges toward the end of the relationship with a narcissistic abuser. This is when you may break the no-contact rule, seeking acceptance and validation from the narcissistic abuser. You may convince yourself that changing or doing things differently could lead to a reconciliation.

This stage can prolong the healing process as you struggle to let go.

Stage 7: Acceptance

The final stage is acceptance. It's the point where you acknowledge your reality and the gravity of the situation. This acceptance marks the beginning of genuine healing. You recognize that the narcissistic abuser is unlikely to change, and it's time to prioritize your own well-being. This is the stage where true recovery and self-empowerment can flourish.

After navigating the above seven stages of and firming reside in acceptance, the following seven stages are pivotal in healing:

1. Going No Contact or Gray Rock Method:

If possible, going no contact with the narcissistic abuser is the most effective way for you to break free from their toxic influence. This means cutting off all forms of communication and severing ties completely. This process can be challenging due to the trauma bond that may have developed, but it is incredibly necessary. While you're in the process of going no contact, you may find yourself ruminating, experiencing physical symptoms akin to withdrawal from a drug, feeling intense grief, blaming yourself, or even fearing that you may never find love again. It's essential to urge yourself to stick through it. Once you emerge from the fog of the trauma bond (which may take several months), you'll begin to notice manipulation and lose the emotional connection you had with your narcissistic abuser. I promise you, there is healing on the other side. In situations where total separation is not feasible, such as co-parenting, implementing the Gray Rock method can be helpful. This strategy involves becoming emotionally unresponsive and uninteresting to the narcissist, minimizing engagement, and avoiding sharing personal information.

Trauma Bonds:

What is a trauma bond? Psychological abuse thrives on destabilizing your sense of reality. The distorted view of the abuser becomes your distorted reality, leading to a loss of confidence in your ability to discern loving behavior from manipulation. You become entangled in their web of control, desperately seeking validation and clinging to the intermittent moments of love they offer after mistreatment, creating what is known as a trauma bond. This bond, fueled by the cycle of love bombing and devaluation, ensnares you in a web of confusion, leaving you emotionally and mentally trapped. But there's more to it than that.

The love bombing after abuse can create chemicals in your brain like cortisol followed by dopamine and oxytocin once the abuser love bombs following an abusive event. These interchanging chemicals can leave you feeling addicted to the abuser even after the relationship has ended. The intricate dynamics that fuel an individual's "addiction" to their abuser are driven by a complex interplay of neurochemical factors. The profound influence of these neurochemicals in dysregulated states makes it exceptionally challenging for you to navigate your emotions or make rational decisions in these relationships, causing confusion and emotional attachment, which makes it difficult for an abusive partner to leave their relationship.

The abuser, being critical, demanding, and abusive, is also at times warm, engaged, and seemingly empathetic and loving. You feel very grateful toward the abuser when they are this way, and as a result, you feel close to the abuser. You work hard to keep the abuser this way, hoping that if you can just be good enough, the abuser will continue to love you and treat you well.

Abusers know just how far they can push you before backing off and then switching to loving behavior. Abuse is gradual, and the stakes incrementally get higher. The abuser knows how far they pushed you the previous time. This tells the abuser that they can get away with that same behavior again. After they have successfully asserted their dominance, the abuser can ease off and use their charming ways to keep you off-balance.

2. Delayed Realization:

Survivors of narcissistically organized relationships often undergo a phenomenon known as "Delayed Realization." It is when you can finally recognize the extent of mistreatment you endured only after you've distanced yourself from the abuser for a significant period. Delayed Realization refers to the gradual awakening to the true nature of the abuse you experienced. Despite leaving the relationship, trauma bonding and cognitive dissonance often cloud your perception, preventing you from fully comprehending the depth of mistreatment until a considerable time has passed.

Realization can be a significant turning point for you, as it marks the beginning of your healing journey. Armed with knowledge and the understanding that you were a victim of abuse, you can seek appropriate support, therapy, and engage in self-care practices to rebuild your life and regain your self-worth.

3. Breaking Free from the Trauma Bond:

As described earlier, a trauma bond is a complex emotional attachment that develops between an abusive individual and their victim. It is characterized by intermittent reinforcement, where moments of affection and kindness are interspersed with manipulation and abuse. It quite literally creates a chemical reaction in your mind of dopamine and cortisol, which is why breaking free may become so difficult. Breaking free from this bond requires recognizing the unhealthy patterns, understanding the power dynamics at play, and actively working towards detaching yourself emotionally.

Another method you can try is writing down the abuse. Make a list of all the abusive behaviors you experienced and reference that list often. Additionally, no contact or extremely low contact is a crucial step in the healing process for survivors of narcissistically organized relationships. By cutting off all contact with the abuser, you create space to remove yourself from the fog and essentially "detox" from the relationship. It allows you to regain independence, truly see the abuser for who they are, and rebuild your sense of self. This physical and emotional distance enables clarity and perspective facilitating the realization of the abuse endured.

4. Healing Cognitive Dissonance:

Cognitive dissonance occurs when there is a stark contrast between the image of the narcissistic abuser portrayed during love bombing and idealization and their true abusive nature. Healing from this dissonance involves accepting the reality that the "nice guy" or "nice girl" you fell in love with was merely a façade. It requires embracing the truth that their actions and behaviors were not a reflection of your worth or deservingness. It's not that there is a Dr. Jekyll and Mr. Hyde. It was that there has always only been a Mr. Hyde who was pretending to be a Dr. Jekyll.

5. Seeking Professional Support:

Engaging with trauma-informed professionals, coaches, and therapists who have a deep understanding of abuse dynamics and its effects is invaluable on your healing journey. They can provide specialized support tailored to your needs, helping you navigate the complexities of healing and rebuilding your life. After narcissistically abusive relationships, you may also experience PTSD/CPTSD symptoms which can be challenging to navigate and process on your own. Having a non-judgmental space to process your emotions, address lingering trauma, develop coping strategies, and soothe your nervous system is crucial.

6. Connecting with Other Survivors:

Connecting with other survivors of narcissistically abusive relationships can foster a sense of community and belonging. Sharing your experiences with others who have gone through similar ordeals can provide validation that your experience is not so unique, you may begin to see your experiences reflected in the stories they tell. Online forums, social media, support groups, or community organizations dedicated to healing from abuse can offer a safe space to share, learn, and grow together.

7. Speaking Up and Raising Awareness:

If you feel comfortable and empowered to do so, speaking up about your experience and using your voice to raise awareness can be a healing and transformative step. Sharing your story not only helps you reclaim your power but also sheds light on the realities of narcissistically organized relationships, potentially helping others recognize and escape similar situations. By advocating for change and raising awareness, you contribute to breaking the cycle of abuse and fostering a supportive environment for survivors.

Healing takes time, patience, and self-compassion. Each step you take towards healing is significant, and progress may not always be linear. Trust your instincts, prioritize self-care, and surround yourself with a support system that uplifts and empowers you.

Chapter 23

References, Resources & Further Reading

If you find echoes of your own experiences within the realms of narcissism, I would like to share a few resources that may offer guidance and support:

- *"The Covert Passive-Aggressive Narcissist"* By: Debbie Mirza
- *"The Covert Narcissist: Recognizing the Most Dangerous Subtle Form of Narcissism and Recovering from Emotionally Abusive Relationships"* By: Dr.Theresa J. Covert
- *"Women Who Love Psychopaths"* By: Sandra L. Brown, M.A.
- *"Malignant Self-Love: Narcissism Revisited"* By: Prof. Sam Vaknin
- *"Why Does He Do That?: Inside the Minds of Angry and Controlling Men"* By: Lundy Bancroft
- *"When loving Him Is Hurting You"* By: Dr. David Hawkins

- My own articles covering narcissistically organized relationships and individuals: medium.com/@elenisagredos

References:

1. Konrath, Sara H. "Empathy: College Students Don't Have as Much as They Used To." University of Michigan, 27 May 2010, https://news.umich.edu/empathy-college-students-don-t-have-as-much-as-they-used-to/.

2. Schneider, Andrea, LCSW. "Idealize, Devalue, Discard: The Dizzying Cycle of Narcissism." GoodTherapy.org, 25 Mar. 2015, https://www.goodtherapy.org/blog/idealize-devalue-discard-the-dizzying-cycle-of-narcissism-0325154.

3. Katzman, Martin A., et al. "Adult ADHD and Comorbid Disorders: Clinical Implications of a Dimensional Approach." BMC Psychiatry, vol. 17, 2017, p. 302. Published online Aug 22, 2017. https://www.ncbi.nlm.nih.gov/pmc/articles/PMC5567978/

4. Baskin-Sommers, Arielle, et al. "Empathy in narcissistic Personality Disorder: From Clinical and Empirical Perspectives." PubMed Central (PMC), 10 Feb. 2014, https://www.ncbi.nlm.nih.gov/pmc/articles/PMC4415495/.

5. Exploring the Relationship Between Domestic Violence and Chronic Health Conditions. Verizon Foundation. http://www.ncdsv.org/Verizon-More_Exploring-the-Relationship-between-DV-and-Chronic-Health-Conditions-survey-summary_10-2013.pdf

6. Czarna, Anna Z., et al. "Narcissism and Emotional Contagion: Do Narcissists 'Catch' the Emotions of Others?" Social Psychological and Personality Science, November 2015. Authors: Anna Z. Czarna, Jagiellonian University, Monika Wrobel, University of Lodz,

Michael Dufner, Universität Witten/Herdecke, Virgil Zeigler-Hill, Oakland University, https://www.researchgate.net/publication/267202488_Narcissism_and_Emotional_Contagion_Do_Narcissists_Catch_the_Emotions_of_Others.

7. Rakovec-Felser, Zlatka. "Domestic Violence and Abuse in Intimate Relationship from Public Health Perspective." PubMed Central (PMC), 2016, https://www.ncbi.nlm.nih.gov/pmc/articles/PMC4768593/.

8. Raveesh, B. N., et al. "Domestic Violence Current Legal Status: Psychiatric Evaluation of Victims and Offenders." PubMed Central (PMC), Mar. 2022, https://www.ncbi.nlm.nih.gov/pmc/articles/PMC9122131/.Rave esh, B. N., et al. "Domestic Violence Current Legal Status: Psychiatric Evaluation of Victims and Offenders." PubMed Central (PMC), Mar. 2022, https://www.ncbi.nlm.nih.gov/pmc/articles/PMC9122131/.

9. Mosquera, Dolores, and Anabel Gonzalez. "Narcissism as a Consequence of Trauma and Early Experiences." European Society for Trauma and Dissociation, https://estd.org/narcissism-consequence-trauma-and-early-experi ences.

10. Hawkins, David. "The Obsessive Compulsive Narcissist." YouTube, uploaded by Dr. David Hawkins, https://www.youtube.com/watch?v=jqI4jE_hqrw.

11. Hammock, Lee. "The Reason Some Narcissists Just Stare at You When/If You Cry." YouTube, uploaded by Lee Hammock, https://www.youtube.com/watch?v=-jb6aJwBtQo.

12. Murphy, Clare, PhD. "Psychological Abuse Wheel." NZFVC (New Zealand Family Violence Clearinghouse), https://nzfvc.org.nz/sites/nzfvc.org.nz/files/Clare_Murphy.pdf.

13. Matthies, S., & Philipsen, A. (2016). Comorbidity of Personality Disorders and Adult Attention Deficit Hyperactivity Disorder

(ADHD)–Review of Recent Findings. Current psychiatry reports, 18(4), 33. https://doi.org/10.1007/s11920-016-0675-4

14. Garfield, David A.S. "Paranoid Phenomena and Pathological Narcissism." PubMed, National Center for Biotechnology Information, 1991 Apr, https://pubmed.ncbi.nlm.nih.gov/2069198/.

15. Conger, Indigo Stray. "Uncovering The Surprising Link Between Erectile Dysfunction And Narcissism… And What It Reveals About Impotence Treatment." Mindsplain, https://mindsplain.com/erectile-dysfunction-and-narcissism/

16. Ettensohn, Mark, Dr. "Narcissism Part 1: The Problem with NPD." YouTube, uploaded by Dr. Mark Ettensohn, https://www.youtube.com/watch?v=I2fD65wy48I.

17. Malkin, Craig, Dr. "Narcissistic, Psychopathic, and Borderline Personalities: Key Differences." YouTube, uploaded by Dr. Craig Malkin, https://www.youtube.com/watch?v=awo-nZItOXI&t=77s.

About The Author:

Eleni is a survivor, abuse educator, narcissistic relationship recovery coach and author dedicated to empowering numerous others who've experienced toxic and abusive relationships through her online platforms and written articles. Prior to her personal encounter with a narcissistic relationship, Eleni focused on mentoring women in their careers within the tech and gaming industries. Recognizing the unique challenges and experiences faced by women in these fields, she aimed to help them thrive. After her own experience with a narcissistic relationship, they pursued CPD certifications in Narcissistic Behavior and Relationship Psychology, using her expertise to educate and support those affected by abuse. Through her writing and advocacy work, Eleni shares practical insights and knowledge by experts in the field shedding light on the complexities of these relationships and offering guidance for healing and growth.

Made in the USA
Las Vegas, NV
30 November 2023

81860765R00125